SPARKNOTES

Power Tactics

FOR THE NEW SAT

THE MATH SECTION
ALGEBRA

SPARK
NOTES

A DIVISION OF BARNES & NOBLE PUBLISHING

Copyright © 2005 by Spark Educational Publishing

All rights reserved. No part of this book may be used or reproduced in any manner whatsoever without the written permission of the Publisher.

SPARKNOTES is a registered trademark of SparkNotes LLC.

Spark Educational Publishing
A Division of Barnes & Noble Publishing
120 Fifth Avenue
New York, NY 10011

ISBN 1-4114-0277-4

Please submit changes or report errors to www.sparknotes.com/errors.

Printed and bound in Canada.

SAT is the registered trademark of the College Entrance Examination Board, which was not involved in the production of, and does not endorse this product.

Written by Brian Higginbotham

CONTENTS

Introduction 4

About the New SAT 5

A User's Guide 8

The Power Tactics 9

Anatomy of SAT Algebra 10

Essential Concepts 15

Essential Strategies 33

Test-Taking Strategies 52

The 8 Most Common Mistakes 56

Conclusion 57

The Practice Sets 59

Practice Set 1: Multiple Choice 60

Answers & Explanations 66

Practice Set 2: Grid-Ins 77

Answers & Explanations 78

INTRODUCTION

Truly effective SAT preparation doesn't need to be painful or time consuming. SparkNotes' *Power Tactics for the New SAT* is proof that powerful test preparation can be streamlined so that you study only what you need. Instead of toiling away through a 700-page book or an expensive six-week course, you can choose the *Power Tactics* book that gets you where you want to be a lot sooner.

Perhaps you're Kid Math, the fastest number-slinger this side of the Mississippi, but a bit of a bumbler when it comes to words. Or maybe you've got the verbal parts down but can't seem to manage algebraic functions. SparkNotes' *Power Tactics for the New SAT* provides an extremely focused review of every component on the new SAT, so you can design your own program of study.

If you're not exactly sure where you fall short, log on to **testprep.sparknotes.com/powertactics** and take our free diagnostic SAT test. This test will pinpoint your weaknesses and reveal exactly where to focus.

Since you're holding this book in your hands, it's pretty likely that SAT algebra is giving you trouble. You've made the right decision, because in a few short hours, you will have mastered this part of the exam. No sweat, no major investment of time or money, no problem.

So, let's not waste any time. Go forth and conquer SAT algebra so you can get on with the *better parts* of your life!

ABOUT THE NEW SAT

THE OLD

The SAT, first administered in 1926, has undergone a thorough restructuring. For the last ten years, the SAT consisted of two sections: Verbal and Math. The Verbal section contained Analogies, Sentence Completions, and Critical Reading passages and questions. The Math section tested arithmetic, algebra, and geometry, as well as some probability, statistics, and data interpretation.

You received one point for each correct answer. For most questions, a quarter of a point was deducted for each incorrect answer. This was called the "wrong-answer penalty," which was designed to neutralize random guessing. If you simply filled in the bubble sheet at random, you'd likely get one-fifth of the items correct, given that each item has five answer choices (excluding student-produced–response items). You'd also get four-fifths of the items wrong, losing $4 \times \frac{1}{4}$, or 1 point for the four incorrectly answered items. Every time you determined an answer choice was wrong, you'd improve your odds by beating the wrong-answer penalty. The net number of points (less wrong-answer penalties) was called the "raw score."

Raw score = # of correct answers – $(\frac{1}{4} \times$ # of wrong answers)

That score was then converted to the familiar 200–800 "scaled score."

THE NEW

For 2005, the SAT added a Writing section and an essay, changed the name *Verbal* to *Critical Reading* and added algebra II content to the Math section. The following chart compares the old SAT with the new SAT:

Old SAT	New SAT
Verbal	**Critical Reading**
Analogies	*Eliminated*
Sentence Completions	Sentence Completions
Long Reading Passages	Long Reading Passages
Paired Reading Passages	Paired Reading Passages
	Short Reading Passages
Math—Question Types	
Multiple Choice	Multiple Choice
Quantitative Comparisons	*Eliminated*
Student-produced Responses	Student-produced Responses
Math—Content Areas	
Numbers & Operations	Numbers & Operations
Algebra I	Algebra I
	Algebra II
Geometry	Geometry
Data Analysis, Statistics & Probability	Data Analysis, Statistics & Probability
	Writing
	Identifying Sentence Errors
	Improving Sentences
	Improving Paragraphs
	Essay
Total Time: 3 hours	*Total Time*: 3 hours, 45 minutes
Maximum Scaled Score: 1600	*Maximum Scaled Score*: 2400 Separate Essay Score (2–12)

The scoring for the test is the same, except that the Writing section provides a third 200–800 scaled score, and there is now a separate essay score. The wrong-answer penalty is still in effect.

NEW PACKAGE, OLD PRODUCT

While the test has changed for test-*takers*, it has not changed all that much from the test-*maker*'s point of view. The Educational Testing Service (ETS) is a nonprofit institute that creates the SAT for The College Board. Test creation is not as simple a task as you might think. Any standardized test question has to go through a rigorous series of editorial reviews and statistical studies before it can be released to the public. In fact, that's why the old SAT featured a seventh, unscored, experimental section: new questions were introduced and tested out in these sections. ETS "feeds" potential questions to its test-takers to measure the level of difficulty. Given the complex and lengthy process of developing new questions, it would be impossible for ETS to introduce *totally* new question types or make major changes to existing question types.

Now that you know these facts, the "new" SAT will start to make more sense. The changes are neither random nor unexpected. Actually, the only truly *new* question type on the SAT is the short reading passage followed by a couple of questions. However, the skills tested and strategies required are virtually identical to the tried-and-true long reading-passage question type. All other additions to the test consist of new *content* rather than new *question types*. Both multiple-choice and student-produced–response math questions ("grid-ins") now feature algebra II concepts. Same question type, new content. Critical Reading features one fiction passage per test, as well as questions on genre, rhetorical devices, and cause and effect. Same question type, different content.

Even the much-feared new Writing section is in a sense old news. Both the PSAT and the SAT II Writing tests have featured exactly the same multiple-choice question types for years. The essay format and scoring rubric are virtually identical to those of the SAT II Writing test. The College Board had no other choice, given how long the test-development process is.

The other major changes are omissions, not additions: Quantitative Comparisons and Analogies have been dumped from the test.

So in a nutshell, ETS has simply attached an SAT II Writing test to the old SAT, dropped Analogies and Quantitative Comparisons, added some algebra II content and short reading passages, and ensured that some fiction and fiction-related questions are included. That's it.

A USER'S GUIDE

Reading this book will maximize your score on SAT algebra questions. We've divided up your study into two sections: **Power Tactics** and **Practice Sets**. The Power Tactics will provide you with important concepts and strategies you'll need to tackle SAT algebra. The Practice Sets will give you an opportunity to apply what you learn to SAT questions. To achieve your target score, you'll learn:

- The two question types you'll encounter: multiple-choice and student-produced response; as well as the subtypes: **Bunch o' Numbers & Letters**, **Storytime Algebra**, and **Obey the Function**!
- What the test-makers are actually trying to test with each algebra question type.
- Essential concepts and powerful step methods to maximize your score.
- Test-taking strategies that allow you to approach each section with the best possible mindset.
- The 8 most common mistakes and how to avoid them.

In order to get the most out of this book:

- Make sure to read each section thoroughly and carefully.
- Don't skip the Guided Practice questions.
- Read all explanations to all questions.
- Go to **testprep.sparknotes.com/powertactics** for a free full-length diagnostic **pretest**. This test can help you determine your strengths and weaknesses for algebra and for the entire SAT.
- Go to back to our website after you complete this book to take a **posttest**. This posttest will tell you how well you've mastered SAT algebra and what topics you still need to review.

THE POWER TACTICS

ANATOMY OF SAT ALGEBRA

Even without reading this book or preparing for the SAT in any way, you'd still get some algebra problems right. However, there's a big difference between:

1. Sweating out a problem, breathing a sigh of relief when you finish, and timidly moving on.

2. Answering a problem, seeing that the next problem contains a herd of easily manipulated variables, and licking your chops in expectation of an easy kill.

You don't want to be sweating through each question. You want to be an elegant test-taking animal, a destroyer of SATs and all algebra questions therein. It isn't as hard as you might think to unlock your inner Algebra Ace. The mistake many students make is taking the SAT cold. That's right—no preparation—not so much as a flip through the information booklet.

By familiarizing yourself with every type of algebra question you can encounter on the SAT, you can approach each algebra question coolly and calmly, knowing in advance what needs to be done to answer it correctly. It's about switching from survival mode to attack mode. It's attack mode that will help you score high.

In this section we provide you with an X-ray of SAT algebra. Later on, we'll review the subtypes of questions and specific strategies for approaching each one. By looking at these questions inside and out, you'll know more about how The College Board tests your skills and how to approach each and every problem you'll encounter on the test.

There are two types of math questions on the SAT: multiple-choice and student-produced response.

MULTIPLE CHOICE

Here is a typical multiple-choice question and the terms we'll use to refer to its various parts:

4. If $a^2 = \sqrt{b}$ and $a = -8$, what does b equal?

    (A) -8
    (B) $4\sqrt{2}$
    (C) 8
    (D) 64
    (E) $4{,}096$

The sentence containing the question is the **stem**. The lettered options below the stem are the **answer choices**. Numerical answer choices are always listed in order from smallest to largest or largest to smallest. Only one of these answer choices is correct. The other four answers are called **distractors**, because that's exactly what they're designed to do: *distract* attention from the correct answer. The stem and answer choices grouped together is called an **item**. An entire multiple-choice section, comprised of several items, is called a **set**.

STUDENT-PRODUCED RESPONSE

Student-produced response is The College Board's way of saying, "Do it yourself, Bub." Simply put, you, the student, must supply the correct answer without choosing from a group of answer choices. Answering student-produced responses requires filling in a grid like the one shown below. Therefore, we will refer to these items as **grid-ins**:

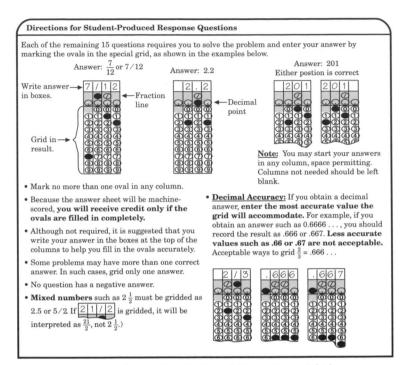

An example of a question in the grid-in section might be:

4. If $a^2 = \sqrt{b}$ and $a = -8$, what does b equal?

It's the same question as before, except that the answer choices have gone to the beach.

The grid is fairly self-explanatory. If you work out an item and the answer is 2, write "2" in the space, then fill in the "2" oval underneath. There are also decimal points and fraction bars in case your answer is not a whole number. We refer to an individual grid-in as an **item**. A complete grid-in section comprised of items is called a **set**.

There are three peculiar things about grid-ins:

1. **There may be more than one correct answer to each item.** You're probably stuck in the "only one correct choice" mindset brought on by excessive multiple-choice preparation. But don't let this paralyze you: if you get more than one correct answer, pick one, grid it in, and move on to the next item.

2. **Answers can never be negative numbers.** Although there is more than one possible answer, there is actually a limit to what you can grid in.

There is no way to denote negative numbers on a grid-in. Why? Who knows, and who cares, for that matter? The fact is that all grid-ins must be positive (or zero, which is neither negative nor positive). So if you come up with more than one correct answer, be sure to choose one that is a positive number. On the item above, if you come up with –8 as the answer (choice **A** on the multiple-choice version), you know you've made a mistake in working out the item.

3. **Improper fractions must be simplified or converted to a decimal answer.** Let's say you come up with $1\frac{1}{2}$ as the answer to an item. If you grid the answer in as $1\frac{1}{2}$, the computer that scans your answer sheet will read your answer as $\frac{11}{2}$. To avoid getting this item wrong, convert the improper fraction into the plain old fraction $\frac{3}{2}$ or the decimal 1.5.

KEY FORMULAS

Multiple-choice and grid-in sets on the SAT provide you with key geometric formulas in a reference area that looks like this:

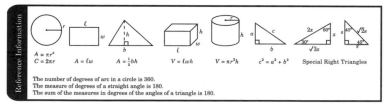

The reference area always appears at the beginning of the set, below the instructions.

WHAT THE SAT COVERS

Algebra items on the new SAT Math section test the following broad concepts:

- Solving equations
- Absolute value and exponents
- Simultaneous equations
- Inequalities and ranges
- Binomials and quadratics
- Functions

Some of these concepts might not be familiar to you. Don't sweat it: that's why you're reading this book!

ORDER OF DIFFICULTY

The number of the item clues you in to whether it's an easy (low number) or hard (high number) item. Sample items in this section have numbers between 1 and 20 that approximate where the item would appear on a real SAT Math section. Make sure to note the number of the item before tackling it. We cover order of difficulty in more detail in our Essential Strategies section.

ESSENTIAL CONCEPTS

If SAT algebra were a radio station, this section would be the Top Forty countdown. It doesn't include every fact, just the ones that get the most airplay on the test. When we describe a concept, we cover only the algebra you need to solve SAT items.

You want to have this knowledge down cold. The better you know it, the easier your life will be. Once you're familiar with these concepts, we'll practice applying your knowledge to real SAT items following our specific step methods.

KNOW THESE TERMS

Skateboarders use words unique to them. So do professional kangaroo wrestlers. Not to be left out, there are special words used in algebra that have specific meanings. Learn these basic six, and you won't be left scratching your head in the upcoming sections. All these words are liberally thrown about on the exam. They're designed to paralyze students who don't know their meaning.

Word	Definition	Examples
Constant	Quantity that doesn't change, such as a number	6, –9, 1
Variable	An unknown quantity represented by a letter	x, y, a

Word	Definition	Examples
Term	The product of a constant and a variable, or a quantity separated from other quantities by addition or subtraction.	$4, g, -8h$
Coefficient	A number that appears in front of a variable and tells how many of that variable there are.	5 is the coefficient of $5t$
Expression	Any combination of terms	$-3, \ r^3 + 8, \ \dfrac{4g - 9 + 17u^2}{5 - \sqrt{g}}$
Equation	Two expressions linked by an equal sign.	$-3 = r^3 + 8$

SOLVING EQUATIONS

At its core, algebra is like placing your coat on the movie seat next to you while your friend goes to get popcorn. People looking at that seat don't actually see your friend. What they see is a placeholder meant to signify that a person is sitting there. If we were to make an equation to represent this, it would be:

$$\text{coat} = \text{your friend}$$

or simply:

$$c = \text{friend}$$

That's what algebra is all about. Letters (**variables**) are used to represent an undefined quantity in an **expression** or **equation**. So in the equation $3w + 6 = 23$, the variable w is merely a placeholder for some real number that has yet to be determined.

Typically, you need to get to the bottom of the mystery and determine the numeric value of w. This is called *manipulating the equation by isolating the variable*. It sounds a bit wicked, but you won't get in trouble for doing it. *Isolating the variable* means you want to mess with the equation until you are left with only the variable w on one side of the equation. An actual number should be on the other side of the equals sign. To manipulate the equation, you can add, subtract, multiply, divide, square, or take the square root of numbers, but whatever you do to one side of the equation, you must also do the other side. You can be manipulative, but you have to be fair about it.

The starting point:

$$3w + 6 = 23$$

subtracting 6 from *both* sides:

$$3w + 6 - 6 = 23 - 6$$

$$3w = 17$$

dividing 3 from *both* sides:

$$w = \frac{17}{3} = 5\frac{2}{3}$$

Ta da! The variable has been isolated, and by manipulating the equation you get an actual numeric value for it.

A majority of the algebra items you see on the SAT will require some bit of manipulation. We can bring back our sample item from the Anatomy section and manipulate it to find the answer.

4.   If $a^2 = \sqrt{b}$ and $a = -8$, what does b equal?

Start with the equation. Here we want to isolate b:

$$a^2 = \sqrt{b}$$

Now we plug in the given value for a.

$$(-8)^2 = \sqrt{b}$$
$$64 = \sqrt{b}$$

Then we square both sides.

$$4096 = b$$

This item brings up a good point. The equation with the variable w is pretty straightforward. Most real SAT items aren't. They are filled with fractions, exponents, and k, where k is a variable representing the kitchen sink. It's all still manipulation, though, so remember to do to one side what you do to the other, and it will all work out.

Distribution and Factoring

These are two nifty little equation-manipulating gimmicks that crop up on algebra items from time to time. **Distribution** takes a term outside a set of parentheses and distributes it across all the terms inside the parentheses. So if you have $6(3w + 8)$, you could distribute the 6 in the following manner:

$$6(3w + 8) = (6)(3w) + (6)(8) = 18w + 48$$

"Great, but so what?" you might say in your most bored, underwhelmed voice. Well, it just so happens that many really complicated-looking algebra items become simpler after distribution. But don't take our word for it:

$$12y^2\left(\frac{y}{3} + \frac{9x}{y^2}\right) = 4y^3 - 72$$

$$12y^2\left(\frac{y}{3}\right) + 12y^2\left(\frac{9x}{y^2}\right) = 4y^3 - 72$$

$$\frac{12y^3}{3} + \frac{108y^2x}{y^2} = 4y^3 - 72$$

$$4y^3 + 108x = 4y^3 - 72$$

By distributing, you now have two similar terms that cancel each other out:

$$4y^3 + 108x = 4y^3 - 72$$

$$108x = -72$$

$$x = -\frac{2}{3}$$

Factoring is distribution in reverse. With factoring, you notice common factors that can be taken out of an equation. Starting with $7r^3b - 28rb$, you can take out the greatest common factor, $7rb$, so that the factored equation becomes $7rb(r^2 - 4)$.

ABSOLUTE VALUE AND EXPONENTS

You can remember **absolute value** by thinking of the two thin upright bars that denote it, $|f|$, as the *Chipper Police*. The Chipper Police are determined that everyone be positive, so no number that comes out from between those two bars is negative.

Any value inside the Chipper Police bars has to emerge as zero or greater. So $|-7| = 7$ and if you have $|f| = 5$, then f could equal either 5 or −5. This either/or ambiguity is what the test-makers like about absolute value, so once you see those bars, alarms should start ringing. There's a reason absolute value works this way. Feel free to look it up if that's your thing. For the SAT, just remember the Chipper Police are always turning a negative into a positive.

This same tricky can-be-positive-or-negative gambit also crops up when you have even-numbered **exponents**, such as x^2 or x^4. Exponents are those raised numbers that show how many times a quantity is multiplied by itself. When you multiply two negatives, you get a positive, so if you have $x^2 = 9$, then x could be either 3 or −3. When rushing through the test or when time is running out, many students jump to $x = 3$ without considering the fact that x can also be negative. Expect this trap to appear at least once on the Math section.

SIMULTANEOUS EQUATIONS

Simultaneous equation items are based on the premise that seeing not just one but two equations causes your brain to leap out of your skull and go cower under a rock. This should be avoided, so let's review.

You will have two equations that contain two of the same variables:

$$2c - d = 31$$
$$4c + 7d = 35$$

Two equations, two variables (c and d), and two methods you can use to solve them:

Method 1: Take one equation and solve for one variable in terms of the other, then plug that into the second equation.

We'll take the first equation, solve for d, then plug that into the second equation.

$$2c - d = 31$$
$$2c - d + d = 31 + d$$
$$2c = 31 + d$$
$$2c - 31 = d$$

$$4c + 7d = 35$$
$$4c + 7(2c - 31) = 35$$
$$4c + 14c - 217 = 35$$
$$18c = 252$$
$$c = 14$$

Notice that we did a little distributing in there, along with all the arithmetic manipulation. Once you have a value for c, you can plug that back into the equation that isolated d.

$$2c - 31 = d$$
$$2(14) - 31 = d$$
$$28 - 31 = d$$
$$-3 = d$$

Method 1 can take some time, but it always works. Method 2 requires a little bit of planning, but it can save you time, so see whether you like it. The key is to answer items correctly, so choose the method with which you are most comfortable.

Method 2: Add or subtract one equation from the other to eliminate one of the variables.

Figuring out how to do this sometimes takes a little manipulating. Look at the two equations again

$$2c - d = 31$$
$$4c + 7d = 35$$

If you take the first equation and multiply both sides by –2, you have:

$$2c - d = 31$$
$$-2(2c) - (-2)d = (-2)31$$
$$-4c + 2d = -62$$

The new first equation c term, $-4c$, would now cancel the c term in the second equation, $4c$, if you were to add the equations together. Let's do just that, then:

$$
\begin{array}{rcr}
-4c + 2d &=& -62 \\
+ \quad + & & + \\
4c + 7d &=& 35 \\
\hline
0 \quad 9d &=& -27 \\
d &=& -3
\end{array}
$$

Once you have a value for d, you can plug it back into any of the above equations to find the value for c, which will once again be 14.

If you set up the equations right, Method 2 can be a bit faster. That's why you should spend a moment viewing both equations to see whether you can figure out a way to cancel out one term. If you can, proceed with Method 2. If you can't, don't waste more time. Just go with reliable Method 1.

INEQUALITIES AND RANGES

When the equal sign in an equation is replaced by a less than ($<$) or greater than ($>$) sign, you have an **inequality**. You can still manipulate both sides of the inequality, and you can still distribute and factor to your heart's content. In fact, there is only one thing you have to remember when dealing with inequalities: **If you multiply or divide both sides by a negative number, switch the direction of the inequality sign.**

Now here's a pop question to test your SAT savvy. Because this is the one weird thing about inequalities, how often do you think it pops up on the SAT? Your answer choices are Never, Sometimes, and All the freakin' time. No hurry. We'll wait.

If you answered "all the freakin' time," bully for you. You're starting to get the hang of the test. You see, almost every SAT item has a catch to it. If you know the catch, the item becomes easy.

Check out the following item:

7. Which of the following number lines accurately expresses the range of x if $-8 < -2x - 10 \le -18$?

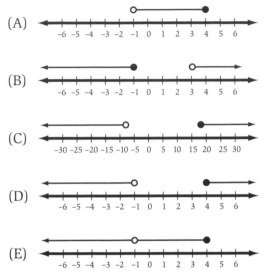

The whole point of this item is to look wacky, because wacky means unsolvable in most people's minds. The long string of numbers and letters is just two inequalities crammed together. If you like, you could separate them into $-8 < -2x - 10$ and $-2x - 10 \le -18$. It doesn't matter. The key thing is to isolate the variable x first. Once you do that, you can jump into the answer choices.

You learned earlier that you can perform any operation on an equation, as long as you perform the same operation to the other side. The same is true of inequalities. It's also true of two combined inequalities. Watch what we do to the string of letters and numbers. To isolate x, we'll first add 10 to each part:

$$-8 < -2x - 10 \le -18$$
$$-8 + 10 < -2x - 10 + 10 \le -18 + 10$$
$$2 < -2x \le -8$$

Now we have to get rid of that -2 in front of the x. Because we have to divide by -2, don't forget to switch the signs:

$$2 < -2x \le -8$$
$$\frac{2}{-2} < \frac{-2x}{-2} \le \frac{-8}{-2}$$
$$-1 > x \ge 4$$

That's the inequality manipulation part of this item. Now you must match what you've discovered with the number line answer choices. Look at the first segment of your answer, $-1 > x$. If x is less than -1, head to the -1 on all the number lines and look for a hollow circle heading left. The circle is hollow because x is not equal to -1, so -1 can't be included. The arrow should head to the left because this covers all the numbers less than -1.

A pass through the answer choices should eliminate everything except **D** and **E**. If you're pressed for time at this point, you can take a guess and move on. If not, all you need to do is look at the second part of your manipulated equations, which states: $x \ge 4$. That single line under the $>$ is the bottom half of an equals sign. It's telling you, "x is greater than *or equal to* 4." On a number line, this is represented by a filled-in circle on the number item. The answer is **D**.

The answer choices for this item show **ranges** of value that a variable can take. Answer choice **D** shows the different range of values that x can have if $-1 > x \ge 4$. Because there's a break between the values x could have, it is called a **disjointed range**. If this range were to go to some range chiropractor and get its joint fixed, it might end up looking like choice **A**. Because choice **A** has an upper bound (4) and a lower bound (right up to -1), it is known as a **single range**.

BINOMIALS AND QUADRATICS

A **binomial** is an expression with two terms. These terms are usually a number and a variable. If you stick your hand in a jar of binomials and grab a bunch, here's what you might have in the palm of your hand:

$$4e + 9, \quad -183q - 1063, \quad \frac{-76g}{3} + 0.75, \quad 2w + 9a$$

On the SAT, most binomials take on the form of a variable (with or without a coefficient) and a number.

When two binomials get together, they really like to party. And by *party*, we mean "multiply all terms together." It's not our idea of a good time, but let's not judge binomials. Multiplying two binomials is like a double dose of distribution. You can use the acronym **FOIL**—shorthand for *first, outer, inner, last*—to remember how to do it.

F = Multiply the two first terms of each binomial together.

O = Multiply the two outside terms together.

I = Multiply the two inside terms together.

L = Multiply the two last terms of each binomial together.

$$(x + 2)(x - 3) =$$

$$\underset{\text{First}}{x^2} - \underset{\text{Outside}}{3x} + \underset{\text{Inside}}{2x} - \underset{\text{Last}}{6} = x^2 - x - 6$$

The expression you get after multiplying using FOIL is $x^2 - x - 6$. If you make this puppy equal to zero, you get a **quadratic equation**. Because the new SAT places more emphasis on binomials and quadratics, expect to see at least a couple of them.

The problem is you can't do that much with $x^2 - x - 6 = 0$. To figure out what x might be, you have to deduce what two binomials combine together to make $x^2 - x - 6$. The kicker is that there's no set, easy way to do this. Where's FOIL when you need it? Well, it's around, kind of. Think of FOIL as a casual friend helping you move. FOIL will move the lamps and silverware, but it's not going to do any heavy lifting.

Look at the first term in the equation $y^2 - 9y + 20 = 0$. Because you know from FOIL that the y^2 is made by multiplying the first two terms together, you can figure out that the first term of each binomial must be y, because when you multiply y with y, you get y^2. Like a puzzle, here's where you are now:

$$(y \pm \text{ something})(y \pm \text{ something})$$

You figure out the next two terms in tandem. Look at the last term, 20, and come up with all the different sets of numbers that can be multiplied together to make 20. Don't forget the negatives, either.

SAT POWER TACTICS | Algebra

Factors of 20

1	20
−1	−20
2	10
−2	−10
4	5
−4	−5

Look at the middle term on this chart, −9y. Which set of factors, if you added them together, would equal −9? The answer's there at the end, −4 and −5. If these are the last terms, then their product is 20 and their sum is −9y. You have cracked the quadratic and now know that:

$$y^2 - 9y + 20 = 0$$
$$(y-4)(y-5) = 0$$

So what is the value of y? Well, the whole equation equals zero, so one of those binomials must also equal zero because anything multiplied by zero is zero. There's no way to tell which one is the culprit, so the answer is $y = 4, 5$.

As you can see, quadratic equations require a good deal of number grinding, and your calculator can't really help you with it. That's why they appear on the SAT.

The Quadratic Formula

This formula is like a first-aid kit from World War I. It should be used only if all else fails. Our previous quadratic equation factored very nicely into the variable y and the integers −4 and −5. If you come across a quadratic equation that doesn't factor neatly, you can still pull out an answer using the **quadratic formula**.

Quadratic equations take the form $ax^2 + bx + c = 0$, where a does not equal zero. The quadratic formula states:

$$x = \frac{-b \pm \sqrt{b^2 - 4ac}}{2a}$$

This doesn't exactly roll off the tongue. In our nice quadratic $y^2 - 9y + 20 = 0$, $a = 1$, $b = -9$, and $c = 20$. Plugging these values in would give us:

$$x = \frac{-b \pm \sqrt{b^2 - 4ac}}{2a}$$

$$y = \frac{-(-9) \pm \sqrt{(-9)^2 - 4(1)(20)}}{2(1)}$$

$$y = \frac{9 \pm \sqrt{81 - 80}}{2}$$

$$y = \frac{9 \pm \sqrt{1}}{2}$$

$$y = \frac{9 + 1}{2}, \frac{9 - 1}{2}$$

$$y = 5, 4$$

As you can see, we get the same answer, showing that the quadratic formula works. As you can also see, factoring is a much cleaner process than working through the quadratic formula.

FUNCTIONS

The new SAT has changed to the way functions look. But the way functions work remains the same. Some makeover!

Functions are like meat grinders, except that you use numbers instead of animal flesh. With every function, you start with an initial number. The function grinds it—that is, performs some mathematical operation—then spits out a finished number. Here's a simple example:

If $f(x) = 4x - 6$, what is the value of $f(7)$?

The term $f(x)$ is what's used to denote a function, and the $4x - 6$ shows what operation you'll perform when you get an input number. Once you're given the 7, start grinding:

$$f(x) = 4x - 6$$

$$f(7) = 4(7) - 6$$

$$f(7) = 28 - 6$$

$$f(7) = 22$$

There it is. You put in a 7, and the function spits out a value of 22.

Those are the basics. That's a simple function, and as you should know by now, when you get to the tougher items on the SAT, nothing is that simple. There are four basic ways to make a function item more difficult:

1. Using a strange mathematical symbols.
2. Using a compound function.
3. Placing the function on a coordinate grid.
4. Talking about the domain and range of a function.

Strange Math Symbols

There's nothing fancy about the first option, except that the SAT will use a symbol such as @ instead of f to signify a function. So don't be alarmed if you see @x: it's the same exact thing as $f(x)$.

Compound Functions

Think of a **compound function** as a pregnant function. If $f(x)$ were carrying the baby function $g(x)$, the compound function would look like $f(g(x))$. What this means is that you have to grind the numbers for $g(x)$—the baby comes first—and once you get an output, you place that number into the $f(x)$ function. Then you can hand out cigars.

9. If $r(x) = \sqrt{x} + \dfrac{1}{x}$ and $t(x) = \dfrac{x^2 + x}{x}$, then what is the value of $t(r(16))$?

Nice and confusing—just the way the test-makers like it. But also quite solvable. Everything's given to you in the item. All you have to do is follow the directions.

Because the r function is inside the t function, you have to run that function first:

$$r(x) = \sqrt{x} + \frac{1}{x}$$
$$r(16) = \sqrt{16} + \frac{1}{16}$$
$$r(16) = 4 + \frac{1}{16} = \frac{65}{16}$$

Now that you have that value, place it into the t function. You can also do a little factoring beforehand to get rid of the denominator:

$$t(x) = \frac{x^2 + x}{x}$$

$$t(x) = \frac{x(x + 1)}{x}$$

$$t(x) = x + 1$$

$$t\left(\frac{65}{16}\right) = \frac{65}{16} + 1$$

$$t\left(\frac{65}{16}\right) = \frac{81}{16}$$

Your answer is $\frac{81}{16}$. You can either grid in 81/16 or convert it to the decimal approximation 5.06, but that's no huge hurdle for you to jump.

Functions and Coordinate Grids

You are probably familiar with a **coordinate grid**, but let's look at one below anyway:

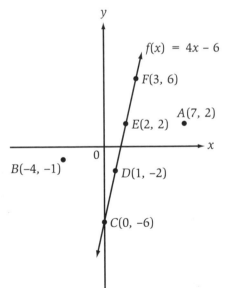

The horizontal line is the **x-axis**, and the vertical one is the **y-axis**. The place where they meet is the origin. Using this system, you can place any point on the grid if you give it an x value and a y value, conventionally written as (x, y). Point A is at $(7, 2)$, and point B is at $(-4, -1)$. The positive and negative values come up because every x value right of the y-

axis is positive, and everything left of it is negative. For y values, all points above the x-axis are positive, and all values below it are negative.

That's Coordinate Grid 101 for you. But you can graph more than just points on a grid. If you have two or more points, you have a **line**.

Now think about a basic function. You put in an initial value called x, and you get an $f(x)$ value. If you call $f(x)$ the y value, you can see how a typical function can spit out a huge number of points that can then be graphed.

Look back to our simple function $f(x) = 4x - 6$. If you put in $x = 0$, you get:

$$f(x) = 4x - 6$$

$$f(0) = 4(0) - 6$$

$$f(0) = -6$$

So $(0, -6)$ is one point you can graph from this function. It's there at point C. If you place $x = 1$ into the function, you get:

$$f(x) = 4x - 6$$

$$f(1) = 4(1) - 6$$

$$f(1) = -2$$

That's point D at $(1, -2)$. You can keep plugging in values and get points like E and F, but there's no need. Once you have two points spit out by the function, you can draw a line connecting them. You have now *graphed* a function.

Some functions will be easier to graph than others. Because $f(x) = 4x - 6$ has no squared terms, it's going to be only a line. More complicated functions might have more complicated graphs, but the basic point is still the same: stick in an x value, work the math and let the function churn out a corresponding y value, then graph that point at (x, y).

Domain and Range

From the previous example, it would seem that functions are interchangeable with equations, but there is a key difference: **for every value of x placed in the function, there can be only one value for f(x).** You can see this easily on a graph.

SAT POWER TACTICS | Algebra

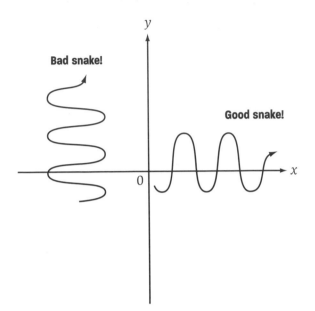

Imagine you're a Samurai warrior. (If you actually are a Samurai warrior, this shouldn't be too hard.) Whip out your function-testing kitana—that's your sword, Samurai—and slice down vertically on the graph. If your blade passes through a line or figure only once, no matter where you slice down vertically, that means there is only one value of $f(x)$ for every input of x. You can try it out on the Good Snake and see this is true. On the Bad Snake, your blade passes through the figure at multiple points. This evil snake is not a function.

Getting back to domain and range, the **domain** is the set of all the x values a function can have. The **range** is the total set of $f(x)$ values that can be generated by a function. Sometimes there are *restrictions* on the domain or range of a function. These are certain values a function just can't have. Consider the function $f(x) = \dfrac{\sqrt{x - 11}}{x + 3}$. If x is any number less than 11, you'll wind up with a negative value under the square root sign. That's bad. Really bad. So the domain of this function is restricted in the sense that x must be greater than 11, or $x > 11$. But wait, there's more excitement to come. Looking at the denominator of the fraction, you can see that if $x = -3$, you would have a zero in the denominator, meaning the fraction would be undefined. That's bad. Really bad. So a further restriction is that x can't equal -3, or $x \neq -3$.

Restrictions on range work the same way. There will be some functions that limit the value $f(x)$ might have. The simplest example is $f(x) = x^2$. No matter what value for x you place in there, your $f(x)$ will be positive because it will be multiplied by itself. So the range of this function is restricted to all positive numbers.

The domain and range of functions are lesser known terms meant to scare you. If you know what they mean, you should be able to determine the answer to an item that asks for them.

Functions As Models

Try this in some open space, like a park:

- Run as fast as you can for 15 seconds.
- Sit down for the next 15 seconds.
- Now crawl for 15 seconds.
- Now run back toward your starting point for 15 seconds.

What have you accomplished? For starters, you should have convinced anyone watching you that you're a bit touched in the head. You have also completed a real-life situation that can be graphed. The "model" of your activity would look like this:

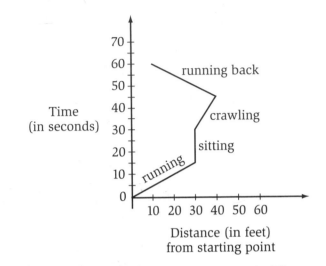

You can see how the model accurately shows each different activity. Because you were running in the first 15 seconds, you covered a lot of distance. Then no distance was covered while you sat on your rump. Crawling moved you forward but not as much as running because, well, you were crawling. Then you ran backward, decreasing your distance from the starting point.

A function as model item will pose a similar question. You might be given a graph and asked which set of activities that graph matches. Or you might be given a set of activities and asked which graph correctly models the activity. Either way, it's a matter of looking at the activity and translating it into graph form.

That covers the algebra basics. Now let's apply these concepts to some SAT strategies.

ESSENTIAL STRATEGIES

Before we dive into the step methods and strategies you'll use on the SAT math section, let's take a look at the types of algebra items you'll encounter on the SAT.

TYPES OF ALGEBRA ITEMS

On the new SAT, algebra items are one of three basic types:

1. Bunch o' Numbers & Letters (hereafter referred to as *Buncho* items)
2. Storytime Algebra
3. Obey the Function!

Here's a brief description of each item type.

Buncho

These are easy to spot. The stem is slap-dash full of numbers and letters (the letters should probably be referred to by their math name, *variables*). Manipulating the letters and numbers so they do your bidding is the key to these items, but this isn't always as easy as it sounds.

You've already seen a sample Buncho item twice:

4.   If $a^2 = \sqrt{b}$ and $a = -8$, what does b equal?

   (A) -8
   (B) $4\sqrt{2}$
   (C) 8
   (D) 64
   (E) $4,096$

Buncho!

Storytime Algebra

These items often have hidden variables, but they can also be clearly spotted by their talkiness. Storytime Algebra items are word problems that either come right out and ask you to set up an algebraic equation or are written in a way that leads you to believe you must set up an algebraic equation to find the correct answer. This assumption—that you have to set up an equation—isn't true, but we'll talk about that later. A sample Storytime Algebra item looks like:

5. Kronhorst has one third as many DVDs as his friend Carlos, who has twice as many DVDs as David does. If k equals the number of DVDs Kronhorst has and c equals the number of DVDs Carlos has, which of the following expressions shows the amount of DVDs David has?

(A) $\dfrac{3k}{2}$

(B) $\dfrac{2kc}{3}$

(C) $6kc$

(D) $\dfrac{1}{3k}$

(E) $\dfrac{2c}{3k}$

There are variables throughout the item, and the stem blathers on for some time. That's Storytime Algebra for you.

Obey the Function!

Old-timey function items on the SAT used only strange mathematical symbols, such as $\Omega x\Omega = 3x$. These looked bizarre but just meant that you were to take any number between the two "horseshoes" and multiply it by 3. These functions were simple. Maybe *too* simple, because these items have been replaced with new kinds of function items. It's survival of the fittest on the new SAT Math section. For example:

5. If $f(x) = 4x^3 - 5$, then what is the value of $f(4) - f(-4)$?

(A)   512
(B)   251
(C)   128
(D)   −10
(E)   −261

Many new functions feature graphs too. If you see an item with a bunch of graphs and no geometry figures around, the best bet is that it's a new function item.

We cover each of the items and provide you with powerful step methods and strategies so you are prepared to answer any item you encounter.

EFFECTIVE STRATEGIZING

Knowing about a strategy doesn't help you if you never use it on the SAT. Many students read a book like this, say "Yes! That's all true!" then never once apply the techniques on the real or practice test. As you might expect, their scores don't improve very much, if at all.

To prevent this from happening, look at every item you encounter and first ask yourself "Which strategy would work well on this item?" Sometimes more than one strategy will do the trick.

The items themselves often contain clues within the stem that give you a good idea of what strategy to use:

If you see . . .	You probably have a . . .
Equations or inequalities with numbers and variables throughout the stem	Buncho
Lots of text describing a real-world situation	Storytime Algebra
Lots of text with variables sprinkled throughout	Storytime Algebra
Expressions with variables as your answer choices	Storytime Algebra
Weird symbols used in an equation	Obey the Function!

The expression $f(x)$	Obey the Function!
The word *function*	Obey the Function!

TACKLING BUNCHO ITEMS

Buncho items are easy to spot, which is good news for you. Once you see an item loaded with variables, numbers, and equations/inequalities, use the following step method to tackle it:

Step 1: Look at the stem and determine which variable or term the item wants solved. Circle it.

Step 2: Look at the equation(s) and locate that same variable or term. Circle it as well. If the entire term isn't present, isolate the variable needed to find the right answer.

Step 3: Write out the equation and start manipulating it—add, subtract, multiply, divide, square, take the square root of, whatever—until the circled variable or term is isolated on one side of the equation.

The reason we use the phrase *variable or term* is because the SAT often does not ask for the single numerical value of one variable. It often asks for two variables together or for one variable with some work done to it. In other words, an item won't ask you the value of x. Instead, it will want the value of $5x$. It does this to trip up students who find what x is, then look down at the answer choices and pick that value. They get the value of x correct, but they get the item wrong because it was asking for $5x$.

Buncho in Slow Motion

Now that you know the three steps to tackling Buncho items, we're going to take you through it in slow motion to demonstrate exactly how it works.

4. If $x^{-3} = 27$, then what is the value of $\dfrac{14}{x^3}$?

(A) 378

(B) 243

(C) 3

(D) $\dfrac{14}{9}$

(E) 1.92

Step 1: Look at the stem and determine which variable or term the item wants solved. Circle it.

In this case, you want to circle the term $\dfrac{14}{x^3}$. That's what the item wants, not x. Sometimes the test-makers do this solely to bust your chops. Other times, however, the unusual term (such as $\dfrac{14}{x^3}$) can provide a shortcut to answering the item.

Step 2: Look at the equation(s) and locate that same variable or term. If possible, circle it as well. If the entire term isn't present, isolate the variable needed to find the right answer.

In this case, the equation $x^{-3} = 27$ does not have $\dfrac{14}{x^3}$ lurking within it. However, you should see quite clearly that the key to this item centers on finding out the value of x.

Step 3: Write out the equation and start manipulating it, until the circled variable or term is isolated on one side of the equation.

Here's where things get interesting. You can solve for x like we do below, then determine what $\dfrac{14}{x^3}$ will be. The toughest step is realizing that

$x^{-3} = \dfrac{1}{x^3}$. This illustrates how the new SAT is all about using exponents and other lesser known math functions to make things difficult. Now solve:

$$x^{-3} = 27$$

$$\frac{1}{x^3} = 27$$

$$(x^3)\frac{1}{x^3} = 27(x^3)$$

$$1 = 27x^3$$

$$\frac{1}{27} = x^3$$

$$\sqrt[3]{\frac{1}{27}} = \sqrt[3]{x^3}$$

$$\frac{1}{3} = x$$

That gives you x, which you could then place into $\dfrac{14}{x^3}$ and come up with the correct answer. However, the strange term $\dfrac{14}{x^3}$ does provide a short-cut. Look at the second line of the equation above, $\dfrac{1}{x^3} = 27$. The term $\dfrac{1}{x^3}$ is 14 times less than $\dfrac{14}{x^3}$, the thing we are looking for. So if we multiply both sides of the equation by 14 at that point, we find the answer we are looking for.

$$\frac{1}{x^3} = 27$$

$$(14)\frac{1}{x^3} = 27(14)$$

$$\frac{14}{x^3} = 378$$

There's your answer. There is no coincidence at all about the presence of this shortcut. It gives you an option if you encounter a Buncho item that does not come out and ask for a single variable. It means you can either solve for a needed variable or you can do a little tinkering with the equation and maybe find a shortcut to the correct answer. Either way, you end up with answer **A**.

Guided Practice

Try this one on your own:

2. In the equation $24 = 3(4x - 12)$, what is the value of x?

(A) −1
(B) 3
(C) 5
(D) 9
(E) 20

Step 1: Look at the stem and determine which variable or term the item wants solved. Circle it.

This item is a little more straightforward. Circling it helps you stay focused.

Step 2: Look at the equation(s) and locate that same variable or term. Circle it as well. If the entire term isn't present, isolate the variable needed to find the right answer.

The variable is standing alone amidst a sea of numbers.

Step 3: Write out the equation and start manipulating, until the circled variable or term is isolated on one side of the equation.

If you get rid of the 3 first, you won't have to distribute this equation.

Guided Practice: Explanation

Step 1: Look at the stem and determine which variable or term the item wants solved. Circle it.

Circling the x at the end of the stem is simple enough. It also alerts you to the fact that there'll be no shortcut or hijinks on this item.

Step 2: Look at the equation(s) and locate that same variable or term. Circle it as well. If the entire term isn't present, isolate the variable needed to find the right answer.

Because there's only one variable, x, circling it in the equation should give you an idea of what you need to do to isolate it. The 3 needs to go, then the 12, and finally the 4 right next to it.

Step 3: Write out the equation and start manipulating, until the circled variable or term is isolated on one side of the equation.

Time to do some math. Write it all out so you don't miss a step:

$$24 = 3(4x - 12)$$
$$\frac{24}{3} = \frac{3(4x - 12)}{3}$$
$$8 = 4x - 12$$
$$8 + 12 = 4x - 12 + 12$$
$$20 = 4x$$
$$5 = x$$

Fill in answer **C** and yell out, "Buncho!"

Independent Practice

After you complete the following item, look at the following page for the explanation.

10. Let $x = 2y$. For what value of z is $(x + y)^3 = zy^3$?

   (A) x
   (B) y
   (C)   3
   (D)   27
   (E)   81

Independent Practice: Explanation

Step 1: Look at the stem and determine which variable or term the item
wants solved. Circle it.

The item is asking you to solve for the value of z.

Step 2: Look at the equation(s) and locate that same variable or term.
Circle it as well. If the entire term isn't present, isolate the variable
needed to find the right answer.

The z in the equation is attached to y^3, so you know you'll eventually
have to get rid of the y^3. But first you have to do some fancy footwork
with the x and the y.

Step 3: Write out the equation and start manipulating, until the circled term
is isolated on one side of the equation.

You're dealing with three variables here, which is a lot to handle. Ideally,
you want to get rid of one of those variables. We know that $x = 2y$, so
why not change the x in our equation into a y term:

$$(x + y)^3 = zy^3$$
$$(2y + y)^3 = zy^3$$
$$(3y)^3 = zy^3$$

Much better. Now you're left with just some pretty basic math:

$$(3y)^3 = zy^3$$
$$27y^3 = zy^3$$

How about that? The y^3 cancels out, and you end up with $27 = z$, answer **D**.

TACKLING STORYTIME ALGEBRA ITEMS

There are two options for solving almost every Storytime item:

1. **The Math Path**—set up an algebraic equation, then solve.
2. **The Backward Path**—work backward from the answer choices to see
   which one is correct.

Both paths work. The Math Path, however, has more traps in it, because
the distractors in the item are designed to trip someone up who takes the
Math Path. It is, therefore, always safer to work backward from the

answer choices. We emphasize the Backward Path because that's the whole point of taking the SAT—to get as many right answers as possible on the test and to do it efficiently. The steps for the Backward Path are:

Step 1: Read through the item slowly.

Step 2: Pick an answer choice instead of a variable. If the item is filled with variables, assign the variables actual numbers so you're working with real numbers, not abstract placeholders.

Step 3: Run the numbers through the necessary computations and see what you get.

Step 4: If the answer is incorrect, pick a different answer choice and try again.

Storytime Algebra in Slow Motion

7. At a popular sandwich shop, it takes 3 minutes for one sandwich maker to prepare a sandwich for a single customer. If lunchtime is from 11:30 a.m. to 1:00 p.m. and there are 390 customers, what is the MINIMUM number of sandwich makers needed to ensure that every customer gets served?

    (A)   9
    (B)   13
    (C)   16
    (D)   21
    (E)   28

Step 1: Read through the item slowly.

The item is tempting you to set up an equation. You can do so if you feel confident, but you're setting yourself up for a fall if you make a mistake. For now, just realize that the answer choices represent different numbers of sandwich makers.

Step 2: Pick an answer choice instead of a variable. If the item is filled with variables, assign the variables actual numbers.

Often, it's a good idea to start with the middle answer, **C**. That way, if you run the computations and come up with an answer that's too large, you can eliminate not just **C** but any answer choices larger than **C** as well. For our example, if **C** were too large, then **D** and **E** would be too large as well.

However, this item asks for the *minimum* number of sandwich makers that could do the job. With that in mind, it might be a better idea to start with choice **A**, the smallest number. If **A** doesn't work, you can move up to choice **B**, and so on. Working the other way makes no sense, because even if you find a large number that works, you still have to check the smaller numbers to make sure they don't work.

Step 3: Run the numbers and see what you get.

Let's try answer choice **A**, which is 9 sandwich makers. Nine employees would make 9 sandwiches every 3 minutes. Lunchtime is 90 minutes total (11:30 a.m. to 1:00 p.m.). So:

(9 sandwiches/every 3 minutes)(90 minutes) = 270 sandwiches

Does this answer work? Well, no, it doesn't. There are 390 customers, and only 270 would get served if there were 9 sandwich makers. So 9 is too small a number, and you know the answer has to be **B**, **C**, **D**, or **E**. If you were pressed for time, you could even take a guess right now and beat the wrong-answer penalty.

Step 4: If the answer is incorrect, try again.

Let's try choice **B**. Thirteen workers could make 13 sandwiches every 3 minutes. So:

(13 sandwiches/every 3 minutes)(90 minutes) = 390 sandwiches

The math works, so that's your answer. Pick **B** and move on.

This process is a bit more time-consuming than you might like it to be, but it's a surefire way to get the item right. If you take the Math Path and make a tiny mistake, you'll end up with one of the distractors and latch onto it.

Guided Practice

Here's a Storytime Algebra item with variables in the stem and the answer choices:

10. Roald has j liters of orange juice that he plans to serve at a brunch. Two-thirds of the juice will go to the adults, who drink r liters each. The rest will go to the kids, each of whom will drink k liters apiece. Which of the following expressions gives the number of children that Roald will be able to supply with his orange juice?

(A) $\dfrac{2j}{3r}$

(B) $\dfrac{jr}{3k}$

(C) $\dfrac{2j}{3rk}$

(D) $\dfrac{jrk}{3}$

(E) $\dfrac{j}{3k}$

Step 1: Read through the stem slowly.

The goal is to find the number of children that can be served. That may mean the number of adults is not crucial.

Step 2: Pick an answer choice instead of a variable. If the item is filled with variables, assign the variables actual numbers.

You have three variables: j, r, and k. Try to keep the numbers small, and make sure that j is a number that can be divided by many different numbers. Also, on this item you may want to avoid the number 1 because anything multiplied or divided by 1 remains 1.

Step 3: Run the numbers and see what you get.

After assigning numbers to all the variables, go through the answer choices and change every one of the choices from an algebra expression to an actual number by substituting your real numbers. Now take those same numbers and run them through the computations required in the item. This should give you a definite number that you will find in the answer choices.

Step 4: If the answer is incorrect, try again.

If you find two choices that both work, pick a different set of numbers and run it through again. If you're pressed for time, you can always eliminate what you can and take a guess.

Guided Practice: Explanation

Step 1: Read through the stem slowly.

Reading the stem, the general trend is that you start with a total amount, subtract the amount that the adults are going to take, then take what's remaining and divide it by the amount each child drinks. That will give you the total number of kids that Roald can serve.

Step 2: Pick an answer choice instead of a variable. If the item is filled with variables, assign the variables actual numbers.

Try this set of numbers:

$$j = 30$$

$$r = 3$$

$$k = 2$$

It doesn't matter that 2 liters per child is a huge stomach load. What's important is that you have a small number, 2, that differs from the adult number. Also, both 2 and 3 divide into 30, which should make the math much simpler.

Step 3: Run the numbers and see what you get.

Let's convert every answer choice first.

SAT POWER TACTICS | Algebra

(A) $\quad \dfrac{2j}{3r} = \dfrac{2(30)}{3(3)} = \dfrac{20}{3}$

(B) $\quad \dfrac{jr}{3k} = \dfrac{(30)(3)}{3(2)} = 15$

(C) $\quad \dfrac{2j}{3rk} = \dfrac{2(30)}{3(3)(2)} = \dfrac{10}{3}$

(D) $\quad \dfrac{jrk}{3} = \dfrac{(30)(3)(2)}{3} = 60$

(E) $\quad \dfrac{j}{3k} = \dfrac{30}{3(2)} = 5$

Now run through the item using our real numbers. If Roald has j liters, then he has 30 liters of orange juice. The adults are going to drink 2/3 of it, so the amount they are drinking is: $30\left(\dfrac{2}{3}\right) = 20$. If the adults drink 20 liters, then there's only 30 − 20 = 10 liters left. If each kid drinks 2 (that's k) liters, then 10 divided by 2 equals 5. That's answer choice **E**.

Step 4: If the answer is incorrect, try again.

You can look at choice **D**, 60, which is way more than the correct answer of 5. **D** is there because it works as a good trap for a student trying to solve this item using the Math Path. By inserting real numbers, you avoid this trap.

Independent Practice
After you complete the following item, look on the following page for the explanation.

3. Eva has just inherited money from her uncle. After taxes, she received a net sum of $32,000. If the tax rate was 20%, how much was Eva's total inheritance in dollars?

(A)   6,400
(B)   25,600
(C)   38,000
(D)   40,000
(E)   45,000

Independent Practice: Explanation

Step 1: Read through the stem slowly.

The dollar amount in the stem is what Eva received *after* paying taxes. That means the answer choices all show what the inheritance was before taxes.

Step 2: Pick an answer choice instead of a variable. If the item is filled with variables, assign the variables actual numbers.

If Eva received $32,000 after taxes, the amount must have been greater than $32,000 before taxes were paid. That means you can get rid of choices **A** and **B** right off the bat. The answer has to be **C**, **D**, or **E**. You should try **D** because it's the middle number of the remaining answer choices. If **D** turns out to be too low, the answer has to be **E** because it is the only number greater. If 40,000 is too large, the answer must be **C**.

Step 3: Run the numbers and see what you get.

What is 20% of 40,000 (answer choice **D**)? $(0.20)(40,000) = 8,000$. Because the taxes on $40,000 are $8,000, Eva would receive $40,000 − $8,000 = $32,000. There's your answer.

Step 4: If the answer is incorrect, try again.

Using our heads to eliminate **A** and **B**, and running **D** first allowed us to skip this step, no matter what the outcome was.

TACKLING OBEY THE FUNCTION!

Rebels don't get functions items right, so take a break from the "down with the establishment" routine when you encounter any function items. Check out the following step method:

Step 1: Determine what kind of function item you have.

Step 2: If there's an input number, run it through the function.

Step 3: Determine whether another number needs to be run through the function or whether one go-through is enough.

Ok. Time to practice.

Obey the Function! in Slow Motion

6. Let the operation $\bigcirc$ be defined such that $\bigcirc r = \dfrac{r^2 - 9}{-5}$. What is the result of $\bigcirc(\bigcirc 7)$?

(A) −11
(B) −8
(C) 8
(D) 11
(E) $14\dfrac{3}{5}$

Step 1: Determine what kind of function item you have.

Just to make things a bit cutesy, we gave you a function item that portrays two different types of functions. It's got a weird symbol, although that weird symbol could be exchanged for an $f(x)$ and nothing would really change. It's also a compound function, because you have to run the function twice.

Step 2: If there's an input number, run it through the function.

That's just what we'll do with the inner, nested function. First, we plug in 7 for r:

$$\bigcirc 7 = \frac{7^2 - 9}{-5} = \frac{49 - 9}{-5} = \frac{40}{-5} = -8$$

Step 3: Determine whether another number needs to be run through the function or whether one go-through is enough.

Like a badly soiled shirt, this item needs another washing in our function machine. This time, we'll plug in −8 for r:

$$\bigcirc -8 = \frac{(-8)^2 - 9}{-5} = \frac{64 - 9}{-5} = \frac{55}{-5} = -11$$

There's your answer, **A**. So long as you do as you're told, functions won't give you any trouble.

Guided Practice

Try this item on your own.

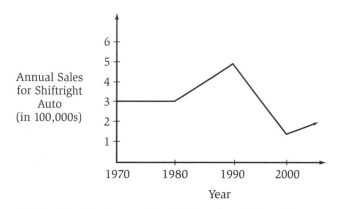

Annual Sales
for Shiftright
Auto
(in 100,000s)

Year

7. Which of the following provides the best description of the events shown in the above graph?

(A) Sales rose steadily in the 1970s, faltered badly in the 1980s, then started recovering in the 1990s.

(B) Sales were stable in the 1970s, dropped in the 1980s, then rose in the 1990s.

(C) Sales remained flat during the 1970s and increased over the next 10 years but have been falling ever since.

(D) Sales rose in the 1980s, fell over the next 10 years, then remained stable.

(E) Sales increased during the 1980s, dropped sharply during the 1990s, then began recovering again in the 2000s.

Step 1: Determine what kind of function item you have.

With the presence of a graph, the answer should come to you. Review the different types of functions on page 26 if you're not sure.

Step 2: If there's an input number, run it through the function.

This is the only type of function that doesn't require the grinding of numbers. In a sense, the numbers have been ground and are already on display.

Step 3: Determine whether another number needs to be run through the function or whether one go-through is enough.

A run-through of the answer choices and a comparison to the graph is what is needed.

Guided Practice: Explanation

Step 1: Determine what kind of function item you have.

This is a Function as Model item. There is a slight chance the graph would throw you off and make you think it is a graphed function, but the answer choices and stem should dispel any notion of that.

Step 2: If there's an input number, run it through the function.

The new SAT added a wrinkle to the old function item. In this instance, you have to obey the function by looking at the chart and finding the answer choice that follows what the chart depicts. We're looking for flat sales in the 1970s, an increase in the 1980s, a decrease in the 1990s, and another increase in the 2000s.

Step 3: Determine whether another number needs to be run through the function or whether one go-through is enough.

A quick read-through of the answer choices is enough for us to conclude that **E** is the correct answer.

Independent Practice

After you complete the following item, look at the following page for the explanation.

5. If $f(x) = 4x^3 - 5$, then what is the value of $f(4) - f(-4)$?

    (A)   512
    (B)   251
    (C)   128
    (D)   −10
    (E)   −261

Independent Practice: Explanation

Step 1: Determine what kind of function item you have.

This is a pretty straightforward function item. The only catch here is that you have to subtract one function from another.

Step 2: If there's an input number, run it through the function.

Let's input our first number, 4, into the function and see what happens:

$$f(x) = 4x^3 - 5$$
$$f(4) = 4(4)^3 - 5$$
$$f(4) = 4(64) - 5$$
$$f(4) = 256 - 5 = 251$$

Lovely.

Step 3: Determine whether another number needs to be run through the function or whether one go-through is enough.

Now let's run through the function with −4:

$$f(x) = 4x^3 - 5$$
$$f(-4) = 4(-4)^3 - 5$$
$$f(-4) = 4(-64) - 5$$
$$f(-4) = -256 - 5 = -261$$

There's your answer, **E**, right? Wrong! The stem asks you for $f(4) - f(-4)$, so you need to take the two values you came up with and subtract: $251 - (-261) = 251 + 261 = 512$, answer choice **A**.

SAT POWER TACTICS | Algebra

TEST-TAKING STRATEGIES

In addition to all the algebra concepts and step methods you have learned, you must also arm yourself with some broad SAT test-taking strategies. If you don't have the correct overall approach to the SAT, all the algebra work you've done will fall to the wayside.

So let's start at a party. Imagine your friends invited you to a cool house party. Hundreds of people are going to be there, and the party promises to be great fun—legal fun, of course. You had to work that day, so you arrive at the party several hours after it started.

When you walk into the house, do you search for your friends first, or do you pick out the scariest-looking person and start talking to him? Unless you like being snubbed, odds are you go through the house the first time looking for friends and other people you know. On a second pass, you might chat with some strangers, but because this is sometimes awkward, you don't jump into meeting them at the start.

PACING

Approach every SAT Math section like this party. On the first go-around, look at and answer the easy, familiar items first. This process is made easier by the fact that every Math section is set up in order of difficulty. The first item is the easiest, the next item's a tiny bit tougher, and so on until the end. A typical twenty-item math set breaks down the following way:

Difficulty	Item Number
Easy	1–6
Medium	7–14
Hard	15–20

Keep this chart in mind as you take practice tests, but also remember that the order of difficulty is simply based on what the test-makers consider to be easy, medium, and hard. You are your own person, and you may find item 15 to be much easier than item 5.

Answering every item in order—no matter how long it takes—is one of the classic SAT mistakes. Students start with item 1 and then just chug along until time is called. Don't be that chugger! If an item takes more than a minute to solve, skip it and move on to the next one. The goal on the first run through of an SAT Math section is to answer the items with which you're most comfortable. Save the other items for the second go-around. Although the next item is statistically a little tougher, you might find it easier to answer.

THE SAT IS NOT A NASCAR-SANCTIONED EVENT

The SAT is a timed test, and some people take this to mean that they should answer items as quickly as possible. They cut corners on items to speed through a section. This is a classic error. It's an especially disastrous policy on SAT Math, because the "easiest" items are at the beginning. If the last item had a fifty-point bonus attached to it, things would be different, but every item counts the same. Getting two hard items right doesn't do you any good if you miss two easy items in your haste. You'll be better off taking the time to answer the easy items correctly, and then using whatever time you have left to take an educated guess on the remaining harder items.

Accuracy counts more than speed. First go through a section and answer all the items that come easily to you. Then:

- Take the time to answer every one of these items *correctly*.
- Take another shot at the remaining items during the second run-through. If you spend two minutes, and the item still doesn't yield an answer, take a guess and move on.

To achieve the second point, avoid choosing the answer that looks "right" at first glance. On easy items, this choice may well be the correct answer. For items numbered 12 or higher, an answer that screams "Ooh! Ooh! Pick me and hurry on!" should be handled like a live snake. SAT distractors are designed to catch the eye of students in a hurry. More

SAT POWER TACTICS | Algebra

54

often than not, an answer choice for a hard item that looks too good to be true is exactly that—*too good to be true.*

Remember, if you can safely eliminate one of the answer choices as being wrong, you should take a guess because you beat the wrong-answer penalty.

For most students, the best method for picking up points in the Math section is by:

- Answering all the easy items correctly.
- Slowing down and catching most of the medium items.
- Getting 25 to 50 percent of the hard items right.

This approach is not as thrilling as getting the hardest five items right (while chancing tons of mistakes along the way), but it does put you on the best path to a high score.

WEAR YOUR NO. 2 DOWN TO THE NUB

There are many students who are afraid of placing smudges on their test booklets. These students don't write down any formulas or equations. They don't write out their work when manipulating numbers. They don't score very well on the SAT, either.

Get over your respect for the SAT test booklet. Write all over those rough, recycled pages. When you are finished, your test booklet should be covered with scrawls, notes, computations, and drawings. In fact, the simple act of writing something down for every item helps improve your SAT score. It forces you to put your thoughts down on paper instead of trying to solve items in your head. If you try to answer items in your head, the SAT will chew you up and spit you out.

Be a smart test-taker. Jot down everything you can.

TAKE A DEEP BREATH AND . . .

Don't freak out when you take the SAT. Sure, the test is important, but many people act as though their entire lives depend on how they do on this one exam. It's not true! It's just one test, and you can even take it over again.

On test day, you want to sit down feeling confident and positive. Do what you have to do to get into that mindset—wear a lucky bracelet, do one hundred push-ups, write love poetry—because you need to believe in yourself when taking the SAT. A positive outlook increases your willingness to take an educated guess on a tough algebra item instead of leaving it blank. It helps you trust your inner ear, enabling you to answer a grammar item, even though you don't know the exact grammatical rule being tested. A positive approach to the SAT is more important than any single fact or strategy you could learn. Banish anxiety from your mind, and all the skills and strategies you've learned to prepare for the SAT will take its place.

THE 8 MOST COMMON MISTAKES

As you prepare, keep the following common mistakes in mind. Some are mistakes to avoid when taking the actual test. Others are mistakes to avoid during your preparation for the test.

1. Forgetting one of the essential algebra concepts. Know your terms and concepts cold.
2. Trying to manipulate an equation in your head instead of writing it down and solving it.
3. Not picking the answer the item asks for. Often this is not the same thing as finding the critical value needed to solve the item.
4. Failing to work through the practice sets in this book—*reading* the book is not enough!
5. Failing to practice the step methods on every practice test item. You need these methods when the answer isn't obvious to you.
6. Refusing to guess after eliminating one answer choice.
7. Answering every item in order.
8. Rushing through a set instead of thinking each item through.

CONCLUSION

Without practice, you won't master SAT algebra. You've learned quite a bit since you picked up this little book, but now comes the hard part—*you* have to apply it to testlike items. There are two practice sets at the end of this book: one made up of multiple-choice items and one made up of grid-ins. Here are some tips for getting the most out of these items.

- **Do not time yourself on the first practice set.** When you begin, don't worry about time at all. Take as long as you need to work through each set.
- **Read the explanations for all items, regardless of whether you got them right or wrong.** This is critical—always read *all* the explanations for each set's items. The idea is to develop skills that help you score points as quickly as possible. Most important, scoring a point doesn't mean you got it in the most efficient manner. The overarching goal is to *apply* the methods you've learned. Whether you get all, some, or none of the practice items right doesn't matter.

After the first set, you may want to start paying attention to time. Certainly by the actual test, give yourself about a minute or so per item.

All the vital information and snazzy strategies you learn in this book won't do a lick of good if you don't use them on the day of the test. Sadly, this happens more often than you might think. Students acquire useful tips, but once the test starts on Saturday morning, all of it goes out the window.

To help ensure that this doesn't happen to you, tackle these two algebra sets *using the skills and strategies you've just learned.* Don't worry about how many you get right or wrong: they're just practice sets. Instead, focus on how well you use the techniques you've learned. When you look at an algebra item, can you tell what method would work best? If it's an Obey the Function! item, what kind of function item is it? If it's a Storytime Algebra item, what variables are in it, and what are some good numbers to use as substitutes for the variables?

Don't get frustrated by your progress on the practice sets. Every mistake you make on practice sets is one that you will avoid on the real test.

Yes, there are some algebra rules you don't know, but learning about these on practice items corrects that deficit. When the real SAT rolls around, you'll have yet another tool in your arsenal that you can employ if needed.

ADDITIONAL ONLINE PRACTICE

Once you're done working through the items and explanations in this book, you can practice further by going online to **testprep.sparknotes.com** and taking full-length SAT tests. These practice tests provide you with instant feedback, delineating all your strengths and weaknesses.

Also, be sure to take the free algebra posttest to see how well you've absorbed the content of this book. For this posttest, go to **testprep.sparknotes.com/ powertactics**.

AND FINALLY . . .

The goal of this book is to show you effective methods for answering SAT algebra items. We hope this helps strip away some of the mystery about the SAT that causes so many students to freak out on test day. You should realize that the SAT is not a perfect indicator of your math ability. In fact, it simply tests your knowledge on a narrow range of math topics. Master those topics, and you will conquer the SAT.

On to the practice items!

THE PRACTICE SETS

PRACTICE SET 1: MULTIPLE CHOICE

1. If $3(x - 6) = 24$, what is the value of $(x - 6)^2$?

   (A) 8
   (B) 14
   (C) 30
   (D) 64
   (E) 196

2. If $12 + 5x > -7x - 24$, what must be true of x?

   (A) $x < -3$
   (B) $x \le 3$
   (C) $x > -3$
   (D) $x \ge -3$
   (E) $x > 3$

3. What is the value of $\frac{3}{2}P$, when $\frac{3}{4}P = 72$?

   (A) 48
   (B) 60
   (C) 96
   (D) 120
   (E) 144

4. A retail outlet is having a clearance sale on all the shoes in its inventory over a period of four days. On the first day it sells 1/4 of its inventory, on the second day it sells 1/2 of the remaining inventory, and on the third day it sells 1/6 of the remainder. What fraction of the original inventory is left for the last day of the sale?

   (A) $^1\!/_{12}$
   (B) $^1\!/_{10}$
   (C) $^1\!/_8$
   (D) $^5\!/_{16}$
   (E) $^5\!/_8$

5. Which of the following lines accurately depicts the function
    $f(x) = -\dfrac{1}{4}x + 2$?

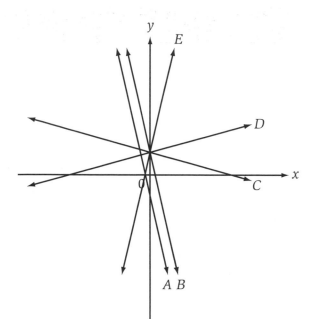

(A) line A
(B) line B
(C) line C
(D) line D
(E) line E

6. If $\dfrac{n}{p}$ is a positive, even integer, which of the following could be true?

        I. n and p are negative integers

        II. n and p are integers; n is an odd integer

        III. $n = p$

(A) I only
(B) II only
(C) III only
(D) II and III
(E) I, II, and III

7. If r is twice the value of p and p is 8 less than s, then in terms of p, what is the value of $r + s$?

    (A) $2(p + 8)$
    (B) $3p - 8$
    (C) $p + 8$
    (D) $3p + 8$
    (E) $\dfrac{p + 8}{2}$

8. If $x + y = 8$ and $x - y = 2$, what is the value of the following expression?

    $$\frac{x^2 - y^2}{x^2 - 2xy + y^2}$$

    (A) 0
    (B) $\dfrac{1}{2}$
    (C) 1
    (D) 2
    (E) 4

9. Train A leaves Romeoville at 8:00 a.m., traveling at 55 mph toward Julietteville. Train B leaves Julietteville at the same time, heading toward Romeoville at 35 mph. If the distance between the two towns is 337.5 miles, what time do the two trains pass each other?

    (A) 11: 52 a.m.
    (B) 11: 45 a.m.
    (C) 11: 32 a.m.
    (D) 11: 15 a.m.
    (E) 11: 04 a.m.

10. Look at the following graph to answer the question below.

Net Caloric Gain/Loss for Person A in One Day

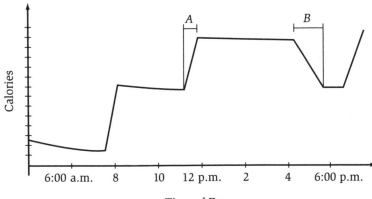

Which of the following activities best describes what occurred during time segments *A* and *B*, respectively?

(A) eating lunch and playing racquetball
(B) having a light nap and taking a brisk walk
(C) having a snack and eating a sandwich
(D) driving in a car and taking a slow walk
(E) jogging 4 miles and biking 12 miles

11. Holly goes to the store to buy peanut butter and jelly for a school picnic. Peanut butter costs $4 a jar, and jelly costs $2 a jar. If Holly spends a total of $28 and buys a total of 8 jars, how many jars of peanut butter did she buy?

(A) 12
(B) 8
(C) 7
(D) 6
(E) 2

12. Stephen is planning to take a two-day biking trip during which he will ride 122 miles. The distance he travels on the first day will be 40 miles less than twice the distance he travels on the second day. What is the distance he plans to travel the second day?

(A) 54
(B) 58
(C) 62
(D) 66
(E) 68

13. In the equation $3x^2 - 15x + 18 = 0$, what are the possible values of x?

(A) 2 and 3
(B) −2 and −3
(C) −2 and 3
(D) −1 and −3
(E) 1 and −3

14. Dana walks from home to school at a rate of 5 mph. It takes her 2 hours longer to walk home from school than it did to walk to school. If her total

walking time to and from school was 8 hours, what was Dana's rate of speed walking home from school?

(A) 3 mph
(B) 4 mph
(C) 5 mph
(D) 8 mph
(E) 15 mph

15. If the function of $f(x) = 2x - 3$ and $g(x) = x^2 - 1$, what is the function of $f(g(3))$?

(A) 13
(B) 10
(C) 8
(D) 6
(E) 3

16. Fifty white-tailed deer in a region are captured and ear-tagged, then released. Six months later, 50 more deer are captured, 35 of which are ear-tagged. Assuming the second group is representative of the deer population as a whole, what is the total population size (rounded to the nearest integer)?

(A) 35
(B) 70
(C) 71
(D) 75
(E) 85

17. Six years ago, June was twice the age of Sue and 8 years older than Bill. If Bill is now x years old, then in terms of x, what is Sue's current age?

(A) $x + 8$

(B) $\dfrac{x + 8}{2}$

(C) $\dfrac{(x - 6) + 8}{2} + 6$

(D) $\dfrac{x + 8}{2} + 6$

(E) $\dfrac{(x - 6) + 8}{2x}$

18. Simplify $\dfrac{9^{90} - 9^{89}}{(3^2)^{89}}$

(A) $-\dfrac{1}{3^{178}}$

(B) 8

(C) 9

(D) 89

(E) 9^{90}

19. Dweezle has $3,500 to invest. He places part of the amount in a stock option that yields 5% interest annually and the rest in a savings account that yields 8% interest annually. If Dweezle earns a total of $238 in interest for the year, what was the amount he placed in the savings account?

   (*Interest = Original Amount* × *Interest Rate* × *Duration.*)

   (A) $700
   (B) $1,400
   (C) $2,100
   (D) $2,800
   (E) $3,500

20. The cells of a certain culture of bacteria double every 6 minutes. If there are 3 cells in a petri dish, how many cells of bacteria will there be after one and a half hours?

   (A) 16,384
   (B) 24,576
   (C) 49,152
   (D) 98,304
   (E) 196,608

ANSWERS & EXPLANATIONS

1.   D

We start off the section with a Buncho item. When you see that the item wants the numerical value of $(x - 6)^2$, bells should go off in your head that there will be a shortcut method to answering this item.

$3(x - 6) = 24$	Divide both sides by 3 and you get . . .
$(x - 6) = 8$	If you square both sides at this point, you have your answer.
$(x - 6)^2 = 64$	There's choice **D**.

2.   C

You should be able to guess why this item is just a little bit tougher than the previous one. It's a Buncho item again, but this time there's an inequality instead of an equals sign.

$$12 + 5x > -7x - 24$$

$$12 + 5x + 7x > -7x + 7x - 24$$

$$12 + 12x > -24$$

$$12 - 12 + 12x > -24 - 12$$

$$12x > -36$$

$$x > -3$$

Because you divided with a positive 12 and not a negative one, there's no need to switch the signs. **C** is correct.

3.   E

There are two ways to go about solving this Buncho item. You can solve for P, then figure out what $\frac{3}{2}P$ equals, or you can try to figure out a way to convert $\frac{3}{4}P$ directly into $\frac{3}{2}P$. We'll skip the shortcut this time and do the legwork:

$$\frac{3}{4}P = 72$$

$$\left(\frac{4}{3}\right)\frac{3}{4}P = 72\left(\frac{4}{3}\right)$$

$$P = 96$$

$$\frac{3}{2}P = \frac{3}{2}(96) = 144$$

There's answer choice **E**. If you want to see the shortcut, look at the two fractions in front of P in the stem. Both have the same numerator (3), so only the dominator is different (2 and 4). If you multiplied $\frac{3}{4}P$ by 2, you would get the $\frac{3}{2}P$ fraction that the item wants.

$$\frac{3}{4}P = 72$$

$$(2)\frac{3}{4}P = 72(2)$$

$$\frac{3}{2}P = 144$$

Choice **E** again. There's almost always a shortcut, but you don't have to find it. You can solve items without it just as well.

4.   D

It's Storytime! The item is pushing for you to create some wickedly convoluted algebraic formula involving all those fractions, but that's a sucker's game. Instead, make up a number for the amount of shoes in the inventory before it all goes down. We're going to use 80. In general, try to pick a fat, divisible integer, and if you have to go to fractions, so be it. Some numbers will work better than others, but if you do the math correctly, it won't matter what you started with. Now run through the computations:

80	number of shoes starting out
80 – 20 = 60	1/4 of 80 is 20, the amount sold on Day 1
60/2 = 30	1/2 the remaining number is sold on Day 2

SAT POWER TACTICS | Algebra

$30 - 5 = 25$	1/6 of 30 is 5, the amount sold on Day 3

So we started with 80 and ended up with 25. This fraction works out to be: $\frac{25}{80} = \frac{5}{16}$, choice **D**.

Just for kicks, try starting out with a different number. Either way, do the math right, and you'll end up at **D**.

5.   **C**

If you have the geometry know-how about lines and slope, you can use that knowledge to solve this item. If not, just place x values into the function that you're given and see what comes out. The easiest number to plug in is $x = 0$, because this will knock out all the stuff in front of the x.

$$f(x) = -\frac{1}{4}x + 2$$
$$f(0) = -\frac{1}{4}(0) + 2$$
$$f(0) = 2$$

Your first point is at $(0, 2)$. This eliminates **A** as an answer choice. Now put another number, such as 4, into the function.

$$f(x) = -\frac{1}{4}x + 2$$
$$f(4) = -\frac{1}{4}(4) + 2$$
$$f(4) = -1 + 2 = 1$$

Your second point is at $(4, 1)$. Only line **C** goes through this point, so it is the answer to this coordinate grid function item.

6.   **A**

Here's a roman numeral item, and you might want to skip these items until the very end. The reason is simple: you have to do the work of three items to get credit for one. For this item, you would have to try different numbers for each roman numeral choice to see whether it could be true.

Let's start with roman numeral III, because it seems easiest. If $n = p$, then $\frac{n}{p}$ will always equal 1. Try a bunch of different numbers and see this for yourself. If roman numeral III is wrong, you can eliminate choices **C**, **D**, and **E** because they all contain choice III as an answer. It's down to a 50/50 shot. Roman numeral I doesn't seem as though it would work, but if $n = -14$ and $p = -7$, then:

$$\frac{n}{p} = \frac{-14}{-7} = 2$$

2 is a positive, even integer, so **A** must be the answer. What about roman numeral II? Who cares? Once you solve the item, move on.

7.   **D**

Here's another Storytime item. As usual, the key is to stop trying to work with abstract values and use real numbers instead. Let's make $r = 10$. The stem states that r is twice the value of p, so p must equal 5. Also, if p is 8 less than s, then s must equal 13, because 5 is 8 less than 13. Write this chart out next to the item:

$$r = 10$$

$$p = 5$$

$$s = 13$$

Now go through the answer choices, replace every p with a 5, and determine the numeric value of each answer choice. The value of $r + s$ is 23, and only answer **D** works out to be 23, so it is the correct choice.

8.   **E**

Here we enter the realm of the medium difficulty items. There's no signpost announcing it, but you have to prepare yourself for items that are a bit sneakier or more involved than the ones you've been working on thus far.

You have binomial terms in the stem and a quadratic expression in the denominator. What do you think the key to this item might be? You'll earn SAT savvy points if your mind jumps to, "There's going to be some factoring involved." If you don't get to this, don't sweat it. You will with some practice. Also, you may want to review page 18.

Once you factor, this item will split open like a sliced orange:

$$\frac{x^2 - y^2}{x^2 - 2xy + y^2} = \frac{(x+y)(x-y)}{(x-y)(x-y)} = \frac{(x+y)}{(x-y)} = \frac{8}{2} = 4$$

Choice **E** is correct. If you don't factor, you can still solve this item if you take the two equations and solve them simultaneously. That gives you values for x and y, which you can then plug into the item. This takes a bit of time, but you can still get the item right.

9.   B

Oh, Romeoville Train, wherefore art thou on the rails? The train item could best be described as a Storytime item, and you can take the answer choices and plug them in to find the right answer. Start with choice **C**. At 11:32 a.m., both trains have been chugging along for about 3.5 hours. In that time, the Romeoville express will have traveled (3.5 hours)(55 miles/hour) = 192.5 miles, and the Julietteville local will have gone (3.5 hours)(35 miles/hour) = 122.5 miles. Let's add these two distances. If they equal 337.5, the trains have passed each other:

$$192.5 + 122.5 = 315 \text{ miles}$$

Choice **C** is a little too short. That crosses out **D** and **E** as well. The answer is either **A** or **B**, and because you need only a little more than **C**, you could guess **B** and feel pretty good about it. To prove it, however:

Romeoville Train = (3.75)(55) = 206.25 miles

Julietteville Train = (3.75)(35) = 131.25 miles

(We used the number 3.75 because that's 3 hours, 45 minutes in decimal form.)

206.25 miles + 131.25 miles = 337.5 miles. Choice **B** is correct.

10.   A

Measuring calories is like monitoring the fuel consumption in a car, because both relate to energy gained or lost. In time segment A, the calorie levels are rising, meaning Person A is "fueling up." What would account for this in a person? Choices **B**, **D**, and **E** all start with activities that would burn calories, so they can be eliminated. It's either **A** or **C**. Choice **C** has the person eating twice. This would lead to a graph showing two upward spikes, not one upward spike and one downward drop. Choice **A** has the person playing racquetball in segment B, an activity that

SAT POWER TACTICS | Algebra

would burn calories and lead to the drop shown in the modeled function. **A** is correct.

11. **D**

If you try to take the Math Path on this Storytime item, you might mess up and get **A** as an answer. This would be quite foolish, because the stem states that Holly purchased only 8 jars total. How could 12 be the answer? It couldn't, but it does work as a good trap for students who mess up the algebra.

Start with choice **C**, which is 7 peanut butter jars. This leaves one jelly jar at $2 apiece. Overall, the total for this mix would be:

$$(7 \text{ peanut butter jars})(\$4) + (1 \text{ jelly})(\$2) = \$28 + \$2 = \$30.$$

We know this is incorrect because the stem states that everything together cost only $28. Too much peanut butter, but not by very much. Cross out **C** and run the item again using choice **D**, or take an educated guess and realize that because **D** is just slightly lower than choice **C**, it's going to be the right answer, which it is.

12. **A**

Here's another Storytime item, and it earns its medium-difficulty badge by being a little strange in its wording. The statement, "The distance he travels on the first day will be 40 miles less than twice the distance he travels on the second day" is intentionally confusing. Even Yoda makes more sense, and he says everything backward. Nevertheless, you can start with choice **C** and hammer away.

Suppose Day 2 equals 62 miles. Twice this is $(62)(2) = 124$, and 40 less than this number is $124 - 40 = 84$ miles. This is the Day 1 travel number. Add the two together and you get $62 + 84 = 146$, which is too much because the stem says the biking trip is 122 miles. You need a smaller number, so **C**, **D**, and **E** are all out.

Let's try Choice **B**, 58 miles. Twice $58 = (58)(2) = 116$, and 40 less than this is $116 - 40 = 76$.

Day 1 + Day 2 = $58 + 76 = 134$. This is also too long. The answer must be **A**. You can check it if you like, but there's no real need. All other possibilities have been eliminated. Hooray for multiple-choice exams.

13. **A**

A quadratic equation appears to test your reverse FOIL skills. Before plunging into the nightmare that is the quadratic formula, try to determine the two binomials. The answer choices will help you, because you can get an idea of what the second term of each binomial might be by looking at what's listed. You can also do a little bit of factoring and take a 3 out of the left side. This makes things even more clear:

$$3x^2 - 15x + 18 = 0$$

$$3(x^2 - 5x + 6) = 0$$

Now factor the equation into binomials:

$$3(x - 3)(x - 2) = 0$$

For the entire equation to equal zero, one of the two binomials must equal zero. So x can be equal to 2 or 3. Circle answer **A**.

14. **A**

Reading a Storytime item slowly can often give you insight into which answer choices are improbable. The story states, "It takes her 2 hours longer to walk home from school than it did to walk to school." If it takes 2 hours longer, she must be walking slower on the way back. That is, she's walking slower than 5 mph. Now look at your answer choices. What can you cross out? **C**, **D**, and **E** are all gone, simply because you took the time to understand the item instead of rushing off to devise the proper algebraic formula.

It's got to be either **A** or **B**. Again, the pull to create an algebraic equation is strong. Resist it. If her total walking time is 8 hours and it took 2 hours more on the way back, there's only one set of numbers that works: 3 and 5. Now maybe you an set up an equation, but only a small one:

(walking rate to school)(time spent) = (walking rate going back)(time spent going back)

$$(5 \text{ mph})(3 \text{ hours}) = (? \text{ mph})(5 \text{ hours})$$

$$(5)(3) = (?)(5)$$

The answer is **A**, 3 mph, because this makes the equation above match.

15. **A**

Obey the Function! In this compound function case, obey function g first, then take this answer and kowtow to function f.

$$g(x) = x^2 - 1$$

$$g(3) = 3^2 - 1$$

$$g(3) = 9 - 1 = 8$$

$$f(x) = 2x - 3$$

$$f(8) = 2(8) - 3$$

$$f(8) = 16 - 3$$

$$f(8) = 13$$

The answer is **A**.

16. **C**

From here on out, you have to earn it. The last five items are going to be difficult, even if you do everything right. For this reason, don't break your head trying to ace all five of these. Getting two or three right and guessing on the rest will still give you a good score, provided you take your time and get the easy and medium items right.

Determining what computations need to be done on this Storytime item is not an easy task. That's just how it is on some difficult items. It's why they're *difficult*.

Fifty deer are caught, tagged, and released. The next time 50 deer are caught, 35 of them have tags. This group of deer—35 tagged and 15 untagged—is assumed to be representative of the deer population as a whole. So the deer population has grown, which means you can cross out at least choice **A**. If nothing else, take a guess from here. But if you have the time to do some math, stick with the item.

The deer ratio of $\dfrac{35 \text{ tagged}}{50 \text{ untagged}}$ is representative of the whole popula-

tion. You know that there are 50 tagged deer total, so

$\dfrac{35 \text{tagged}}{50 \text{ untagged}} = \dfrac{50 \text{ tagged-whole-population}}{\text{?-whole-population}}$. At this point, you can

start plugging in answer choices where the question mark is or you can cross-multiply the ratio to find the answer. The ratio is very close to an algebraic equation, but that can't be helped.

$$\frac{35 \text{ tagged}}{50 \text{ untagged}} = \frac{50 \text{ tagged-whole-population}}{?\text{-whole-population}}$$

$$\frac{35}{50} = \frac{50}{n}$$

$$35n = (50)(50)$$

$$35n = 2500$$

$$n = 71.42 \approx 71$$

C is the answer.

17. **C**

Give June an age now, and you can figure everything out from there. Let's make her 20, so $J = 20$. Six years ago would make June age 14. If she was twice Sue's age at that time, $S = 7$. If June was 8 years older than Bill when she was 14, $B = 6$. We have:

$$J = 20$$

$$S = 7$$

$$B = 6$$

If x equals Bill's current age, then $x = 6 + 6 = 12$. Sue was 7 six years ago, so now she is 13.

Go through all the answer choices and replace each x with a 12. Then find the answer choice that works out to 13. **C**'s your answer.

18. **B**

This item illustrates how you can understand a concept such as factoring, but unless you really, really have a good understanding of it, you won't be able to utilize it on the difficult items.

You might be able to use your calculator to muddle through this, but it won't be pretty. It also might not work simply because the numbers are too large. The real key is to see the hidden 9^{89}s. factor them out, then simplify. To do this, look at the following equation until you see why it makes sense:

$$9^{90} = 9^{89+1} = (9^{89})(9^1) = (9^{89})9$$

We pulled out one of the 9s from 9^{90} to make it $(9^{89})(9)$. This will allow us to take this unwieldy expression and whittle it down.

$$\frac{9^{90} - 9^{89}}{(3^2)^{89}} = \frac{9^{90} - 9^{89}}{9^{89}} = \frac{(9^{89})(9) - 9^{89}}{9^{89}} = \frac{9^{89}(9-1)}{9^{89}}$$

$$= (9-1) = 8$$

Choice **B** is correct.

19. **C**

It's a Storytime item, but computations are going to be involved. Start with choice **C** and see what it brings. If Dweezle placed $2,100 in savings, then $3,500 – $2,100 = $1,400 is in a stock option. The interest on both these would be:

$$(0.08)(2,100) + (0.05)(1,400) = 168 + 70 = \$238$$

Hot diggity, it's **C**! Got it in one go.

20. **D**

This is another Storytime item, but working backward might be messier than going forward. The best approach to this item is to be ready and willing to start writing immediately. In 90 minutes (the hour-and-half time), the bacteria will double $90/6 = 15$ times, because there are 15 six-minute segments in 90 minutes.

Go low-tech for the toughest items. The test-makers won't expect that route, which usually has its benefits. Write out the numbers 1 through 15 on a scratch sheet of paper. Then start figuring out how many bacteria there are. It's as simple as hitting the "times 2" function on your calculator.

Start	3 cells
1	6
2	12
3	24
4	48
5	96
6	192
7	384
8	768
9	1,536
10	3,072
11	6,144
12	12,288
13	24,576
14	49,152
15	98,304

There's your answer, choice **D**. The actual algebra would take some time to explain and would make your skull ache. Finding the answer is what's important, and that's what we did.

SAT POWER TACTICS | Algebra

PRACTICE SET 2: GRID-INS

1. If $a + b + c = -350$ and $a = -725$, what is the value of $b + c$?

$$\sqrt{9} \le m \le \sqrt{49}$$
$$2^2 < n < 3^2$$

2. If m and n are integers that satisfy the conditions above, what is one possible value of $m + n$?

3. The Acme Industrial Technical College has fallen on hard times. Last year its enrollment dropped by 20%, and this year enrollment dropped another 15% from last year's. Next year the college expects to have 50% of this year's enrollment. What percent of enrollment can be expected to drop for all 3 years?

4. If $f(x) = x^2 - 2x$, what does $f(6)$ equal?

5. $(2x - 3)(5x + 14) = ax^2 + bx + c$, where a, b, and c are numerical constants. Determine the value of b.

6. If 35% of 40% of x equals 70, what is the value of x?

7. $4x - 5y = 4$ and $2x - y = 8$. Using this information, determine the value of $(x - y)$.

8. The price of typewriters has increased by $10 per year over the past 5 years. If a typewriter currently retails for $165, by what percentage did the price of typewriters increase over the last 5 years?

9. If $x^2 - y^2 = 48$, and $x + y = 12$, what is the value of $x - y$?

10. Cindy currently has a balance of $240 on her credit card bill. She intends to pay 4% of the balance annually, but the debt has a 5% annual interest rate. After 4 years her debt will have increased by how much, in dollars?

11. The expression $\dfrac{6x-2}{8} + \dfrac{2x+5}{8}$ is how much greater than x?

12. If the function of $g(z) = az - b$, where a and b are constants, $g(12) = 83$, and $g(4) = 19$, what is the value of b?

13. It takes Ralph 4 hours to complete a certain job. Potsy can complete the same job in 3 hours. If Ralph and Potsy work together to complete $\dfrac{3}{4}$ of the job, how long in hours will it take Ralph to finish the job by himself?

14. If x and y are positive integers, $x > 30$, and $x - y > 25$, what is the LEAST possible value of $x + y$?

15. In the function $f(x) = \sqrt{x} \cdot x^2$, the domain is all positive numbers. What is one integer value of the range of this function?

ANSWERS & EXPLANATIONS

1. **375**

This is the easiest item—does it show? It's Beginner's Buncho:

$$a + b + c = -350$$

$$-725 + b + c = -350$$

$$-725 + 725 + b + c = -350 + 725$$

$$b + c = 375$$

Grid in the number 375.

2. **10**

Of the two integers, n is probably easier to figure out, so let's do that one first.

$$2^2 < n < 3^2$$
$$4 < n < 9$$

The variable n can be 5, 6, 7, or 8. One of the weird things about grid-in items is that there isn't always one single answer. We can use any one of these integers and still get credit for this item, provided we determine the value of m correctly:

$$\sqrt{9} \le m \le \sqrt{49}$$

$$3 \le m \le 7$$

Because those are less than or equal to signs, m can be 3, 4, 5, 6, or 7. But don't spend time deciding which value to use. Both m and n can be 5, and $5 + 5 = 10$, so grid in 10 and move on. (Any integer value between 8 and 15 works.)

3. **66**

Poor Acme. Sob Storytime aside, the key here is to come up with a number, then start chipping away at it with the appropriate percentages. Because percentages are involved, it may be very helpful to say that Acme started out with 100 students. Starting with 100 on percentage items often makes it easier to calculate percentage change.

First year:	100 students
After a 20% drop:	20% of 100 is 20, so enrollment is now at $100 - 20 = 80$.
Another 15% drop:	15% of 80 = $(0.15)(80) = 12$ students. $80 - 12 = 68$. Only 68 remain.
Projected 50% drop:	50% of 68 is 34, so there are only 34 students left at Acme.

Because you start with 100 students, figuring out the percentage drop for all 3 years takes only a bit of substitution: $100 - 34$ remaining students = 66 students gone = 66%. If you use a number other than 100, you have to do some more involved computing. So don't.

4. **24**

Obey the Function! There's nothing more to this item.

$$f(x) = x^2 - 2x$$

$$f(6) = (6)^2 - 2(6)$$

$$f(6) = 36 - 12$$

$$f(6) = 24$$

5.   **13**

Here are two binomials begging to be FOILed. Once you send them through the FOILer, all you need to do is pick out b, the numerical value in front of the x variable.

$$(2x - 3)(5x + 14) =$$
$$10x^2 + 28x - 15x - 42 =$$
$$10x^2 + 13x - 42$$

This means that $b = 13$.

6.   **500**

If this were a multiple-choice item, we could head down to the answer choices and start trying different answers. But this isn't a multiple-choice section, is it? That's the whole nefarious point of the grid-in section. It limits the number of strategies you can use to find the right answer.

We have to set up a simple equation instead. If 35% of 40% of x equals 70, then:

$$(35\%)(40\%)(x) = 70$$

Of means "multiply" in Mathspeak.

$$(0.35)(0.4)x = 70$$

Here we convert the percentages to decimals by moving the decimal points two spaces to the left.

$$0.14x = 70$$

Dividing both sides by 0.14 leaves you with . . .

$$x = 500$$

The answer.

7.   **2**

You have two equations with two variables. It's the classic simultaneous equation setup. As you recall from our work on Simultaneous Equations, you have two possible ways to solve this item. Because the second equation is fairly basic ($2x - y = 8$), we're going to solve for y in that one, then place that value into the other equation.

$$2x - y = 8$$

$$2x = 8 + y$$

$$2x - 8 = y$$

$$4x - 5y = 4$$
$$4x - 5(2x - 8) = 4$$
$$4x - 10x + 40 = 4$$
$$-6x + 40 = 4$$
$$-6x + 40 - 40 = 4 - 40$$
$$-6x = -36$$
$$x = 6$$

There's x. You know that $2x - 8 = y$, so:

$$2x - 8 = y$$

$$2(6) - 8 = y$$

$$12 - 8 = y$$

$$4 = y$$

One last computation to go. The item asked for $(x - y)$—did you circle this?—so the answer is $6 - 4 = 2$.

All that work for a lousy 2.

8.   **43.478**

This is another Storytime item that would be much simpler if we had answer choices to pick from. As it is, we'll have to take the Math Path, albeit reluctantly.

If the price of typewriters has increased by $10 per year over the past 5 years, then typewriters have gone up (5 years)($10 per year) = $50 in price. If they are currently at $165, then their price 5 years ago was $165 – $50 = $115.

We now must ask the question, "What percent of 115 is 50?" (Note that you use the original price to calculate percentage increase, not the current price of $165.) In Mathspeak, this item works out to:

$$x\% \text{ of } 115 = 50$$

$$\left(\frac{x}{100}\right)(115) = 50$$

$$\frac{115x}{100} = 50$$

$$\left(\frac{100}{115}\right)\left(\frac{115x}{100}\right) = 50\left(\frac{100}{115}\right)$$

$$x \approx 43.478\,\%$$

Here's one of the funky things about grid-in items. You get credit if you grid in 43.478, 43.47, or 43.48. You don't have to fill in the entire grid, and you don't have to round up or down correctly. In general, though, try to make your answers as precise as possible—it's always best to err on the side of caution.

9. **4**

This is a quadratic item, but it doesn't look that way at first because the middle bx term is missing. To be more precise, the middle term does not exist because it is canceled out.

$$x^2 - y^2 = 48$$

$$(x + y)(x - y) = 48$$

That's the key to this item. From there, you're given $x + y = 12$, so:

$$(x + y)(x - y) = 48$$

$$12(x - y) = 48$$

$$(x - y) = 4$$

10. **9.74**

If you understand percentages, you can take a shortcut on this item. Usually you can't add or subtract percentages because the base value (the value whose percentage is being taken) is different. But on this item, the base value for Cindy's balance payment and debt increase is the same, $240. This means you can combine the two percentages and uncover the net change in debt:

4% payments – 5% debt increase = 1% debt increase per year

1% of \$240 is \$2.40. After the first year, Cindy now owes \$242.40. Now find out the increase for the second year, 1% of \$242.40 is \$2.424; for the third year, 1% of \$244.824 is \$2.44824; and for the fourth year. 1% of \$247.27224 is \$2.4727224. Now add up the four: \$2.40 + \$2.424 + \$2.44824 + \$2.4727224 = \$9.7449624 or \$9.74.

11. **3/8**

The brace of fractions makes this Buncho look much tougher than it really is. Because each fraction has an 8 in the denominator, they can be combined.

$$\frac{6x - 2}{8} + \frac{2x + 5}{8}$$
$$\frac{6x - 2 + 2x + 5}{8}$$
$$\frac{8x + 3}{8}$$

We achieve what is needed by putting the two fractions together. Watch what happens when they are separated again:

$$\frac{8x + 3}{8}$$
$$\frac{8x}{8} + \frac{3}{8}$$
$$x + \frac{3}{8}$$

There's your answer. The expression is greater than x by $\frac{3}{8}$.

12. **13**

This looks like a function item, and it is, but it's also something else. If you write out the two functions given, you have:

$$g(z) = az - b =$$
$$12a - b = 83$$

$$g(z) = az - b =$$
$$4a - b = 19$$

There are two equations with two variables. You have a simultaneous equation situation hiding out. It's tricky, but what did you expect, now that you're in the Land of the Hard Items?

We solved the last simultaneous equation by one method, so we'll use the other method for this one. The *b* in the item above will cancel out as is, but *b* is the variable we're looking for. To get rid of the *a* terms, multiply the second equation by −3 and see what happens:

$$4a - b = 19$$
$$(-3)4a - (-3)b = (-3)19$$
$$-12a + 3b = -57$$

We can take this equation and add it to the first one:

$$
\begin{array}{rcrcr}
12a & - & b & = & 83 \\
+ & & + & & + \\
-12a & + & 3b & = & -57 \\
\hline
 & & 2b & = & 26 \\
 & & b & = & 13
\end{array}
$$

It's an unlucky number, but a correct one.

13. **1**

Picking the right number will really help on this item. You have 4s and 3s abounding, so pick a number divisible by both, such as 12. Let's say the job Ralph and Potsy are working on is chair making. They need to make 12 chairs. It takes Ralph 4 hours to make 12 chairs, so he works at a rate of 3 chairs/hour:

Ralph: (4 hours)(3 chairs/hour) = 12 chairs

Potsy is faster. He takes only 3 hours to make 12 chairs, so his rate can be calculated in your head as 4 chairs/hour:

Potsy: (3 hours)(4 chairs/hour) = 12 chairs

Together, they complete $^3/_4$ of the job. What is $^3/_4$ of 12?

$$\frac{3}{4}(12) = 9$$

That means 3 chairs remain because 12 − 9 = 3. The item asks how long in hours it will take Ralph to finish the job by himself. If Ralph completes 3 chairs/hour and there are 3 chairs left, it will take him 1 hour to finish the job.

SAT POWER TACTICS | Algebra

SAT POWER TACTICS | Algebra

14. **32**

Let's start small and take things from there. If $x > 30$, begin $x = 31$. Moving to the next inequality, $x - y > 25$, the largest number we can make for y is 5. This makes $x + y = 36$, but is this the least possible value? Keep in mind we're looking for the smallest number we can make, so using the largest value for y is not in our best interests. We want the smallest of y possible, and we can combine this with the smallest value of x that works.

If $x = 31$, the largest number we can make for y is 5, but the LEAST possible value for y is 1, because 1 is the smallest positive integer. (Zero is neither positive nor negative.) Having y equal to 1 still satisfies the second equation because:

$$x - y > 25$$

$$31 - 1 > 25$$

$$30 > 25$$

Therefore, the smallest value for $x + y$ is $31 + 1 = 32$.

15. **32**

The last item is quite often the weirdest. No exception here. You have to know about functions, and you have to understand the vocabulary to have a chance on this item. The item wants a range value, and you know the range is the set of all possible values of $f(x)$ that can be generated. You did know that, right? More so, the item wants "an integer value" of the range. This means you can't just plug in some positive x value and write the output down. You have to pick a number that will go into $f(x) = \sqrt{x} \cdot x^2$ and emerge an integer.

The key is the square root part. If you pick a perfect square, your number should emerge from under the square root sign unscathed. Some simple perfect squares are 4, 9, and 16. Let's use 4:

$$f(x) = \sqrt{x} \cdot x^2$$
$$f(4) = \sqrt{4} \cdot 4^2 = 2 \cdot 16 = 32$$

32 is one integer value for the range of this particular function and will work just fine as our answer.

SPARKNOTES
Power Tactics for the New SAT

The Critical Reading Section

Reading Passages

Sentence Completions

The Math Section

Algebra

Data Analysis, Statistics & Probability

Geometry

Numbers & Operations

The Writing Section

The Essay

Multiple-Choice Questions: Identifying Sentence Errors, Improving Sentences, Improving Paragraphs

The New SAT

Test-Taking Strategies

Vocabulary Builder

AS SEEN ON
WWW

EXCLUSIVE TO
Barnes & Noble

Don't bother
...we've done it for you!

la felicidad

Andrew Johnson

Planck's const

aerobi

Sick of scribbling on index cards?

Making that bump on your finger worse?

Relax... SparkNotes has it covered!

SPARKNOTES STUDY CARDS
WWW.SPARKNOTES.COM

U.S. History
STUDY CARDS
600 CARDS

SparkNotes®
Study Cards

not only come in the most
popular subjects, but they also
translate difficult subject matter into
digestible tidbits, making them the must-have studying companion.
And if you still want to write your own cards, we've got blank ones too!

Titles include
Biology
Blank Cards
Chemistry
English Grammar
English Vocabulary
French Grammar
French Vocabulary
Geometry
Organic Chemistry
Physics
Pre-Algebra
Spanish Grammar
Spanish Vocabulary
U.S. History

SAT vocabulary novels

euphoria

effulgent: bright or beaming
mustering: gathering
mortifying: shameful
nocturnal: active at night

ebullient: bright
cheerful
epiphany: sudden
realization or awakening

epiphany

excavate: dig out
discarded: thrown away
meticulously: carefully
thoroughly
euphoria: exhilaration o

Learning
—without even realizing it!

Need to study for the SATs, but would rather read a good book? Now SparkNotes®
lets you do both. Our **SAT Vocabulary Novels** are compelling full-length novels
wtih edgy and mature themes that you'll like (honest). Each book highlights more
than 1,000 vocabulary words you'll find on the SAT. Brief definitions appear at the
bottom of the page, so you can sit back, read a good book, and get some serious
studying done—all at the same time!

excerpts and more at www.sparknotes.com/**buy/satfiction/**

Busted   Head Over Heels   Sunkissed   Vampire Dreams